I DRINK COFFEE AND MAKE SHIT UP

ONE WRITER'S JOURNEY WITHOUT SIGNPOSTS

BAER CHARLTON

Copyright ©2020 by Baer Charlton
I Drink Coffee and Make Shit Up
By Baer Charlton

All rights reserved.

No part of this publication may be reproduced or transmitted in any form or by any means, electronic or mechanical, including photocopy, recording, or any information storage and retrieval system without the prior written consent of the author, except in the instance of quotes for reviews. No part of this book may be scanned, uploaded, or distributed via the internet without the permission of the author and is a violation of the International Copyright law, which subjects the violator to severe fines and imprisonment.

Rogena Mitchell-Jones, Literary Editor
RMJ Manuscript Service, www.rogenamitchell.com

Published by Mordant Media, Portland, Oregon

ISBN: 978-1-949316-14-8 [ebook]
ISBN: 978-1-949316-15-5 [paperbook]

10 9 8 7 6 5 4 3 2 1

CONTENTS

Dedication	1
A preliminary thought…	5
1. Building a Writer	9
2. Getting Started or Chapter 4,783.2b or You Might Call It the Foreward or the Important Chapter You Never Read	77
3. Putting it All Together	81
4. Cozy Confrontation	84
5. A Higher Education	88
6. Family	110
7. A Tougher Education – Adulthood, or Almost	117
8. Let's Talk About Death	131
9. Christmas	144
10. Putting Things Together	151
11. Memories and Other Lost Thoughts	155
12. Putting it all Together	167
13. The Flight Captain's Memory Box	172
14. Another Thought	177
15. Lunch, Coffee, and World Travel	188
16. One Last Thought—Really	214
Baer Charlton	220
About the Author	221

DEDICATION

Here is where most authors write something saccharine sweet and straightforward, like *To my mother*.

But this is where I explain the only signposts in my life. Thank you, Mom.

My wife and I couple-dated some friends we referred to as our Canasta Friends. Even after we moved sixteen-hundred miles away, we would fly down and spend three solid days playing Canasta. Of course, those who play Canasta will tell you there is some eating, occasional drinking (coffee), and much talking with every hand. They told us about their travels with another couple, and we talked about our world travels. One difference was always clear: the nation's border separated our experiences.

During one of the last trips down, he asked why we traveled and spent our money in other countries when there were so many neat places to go here in the states. I asked for an inference. He named a place. He was right… It was a neat place. One of us had been there. He chose another. I told him about the fabulous restaurant I had found there after exploring the region they had not dared to go. He grumped another tourist attraction. I countered about the incredible natural creations less than a day's drive away—I had been there. He named an obscure national park, and my wife rattled off five more within a half day's car ride with three kids and towing a small trailer. She had spent every summer touring all forty-eight states.

Finally, I shared what drove me to distant lands.

Long before I knew of a city named New York, I learned about the city of Paris. Years before I knew about the stockyards of a place called Chicago, I learned about the thick fog of London and the evil done by a Mr. Hyde or Ripper.

New Orleans came long after I knew of Cairo on the banks of the Nile River, pyramids, and the Aswan Dam, thanks to a boy king named Tut and National Geographic Magazine. The Grand Bazaar of Bagdad I learned from a boy named Ali.

I had wandered through the jungles of India with Mowgli, thanks to Rudyard Kipling. The same year I learned about a captivating animal called a mongoose. Africa would come at the fanciful hand and pen of Edger Rice Burroughs. It was through his Tarzan that I began my lessons in Swahili with naming the animals. Denver, Colorado, and the Rocky Mountains would come long after I had also trekked to the Yukon with Jack London and Robert Service.

I learned of the port of Los Angeles, long after I had worked the docks of Cannery Row. I had been Shanghaied in San Francisco and pressed into labor on the quays of Lisbon and Calais. I had sailed around both capes, hunted a great white whale, and sold into slavery next to a shipload of bananas and spices in Grenada.

As a great person once said, to open a book is to step onto a magic carpet taking you anywhere you can read about. Some of the first books I read were the classics. By the age of nine, I had floated over London, danced on the ramparts of Notre Dame, fenced in defense of a beautiful lady in Calais. I had listened to great orators in the Senate of Athens, ridden an elephant while storming Carthage, pilfered goods in Bagdad, and ruled the world from Alexandria. I had sailed a felucca on the Nile, a junk off China, and a stolen Royal Navy ship of the line to a tiny island in the Pacific Ocean still on my bucket list—Pitcairn.

To recognize my mother is also to understand who she introduced us to as children. As she read to us on her bed in the evening, she planted the seeds of reading, between the rows of chenille knotting of her quilt. She planted the spark of wanderlust in the eye of her youngest—to venture forth and then return to write. Experience, eat, meet, and consume, then home again to write.

When I was a young man, my mentor slipped the shackles of the earthly binds and took wing to her next adventure. Years later, my father handed me a small stack of yellow three-by-five cards bound by print shop rubber bands of red and blue. The stack was all the notes of stories my mother and I had created in long evenings performing the tedious task of printing. I tossed the unopened stack into the top drawer of my desk.

A few years later, I was cleaning out the desk. I unwound the rubbers and inserted my thumbnails into the center, splitting the stack. A small piece of yellow paper fluttered to the floor.

As I bent to look, the importance of a single word hit me. It was my total inheritance from her. It was what she couldn't bring herself to try.

She had reached from the grave and directed me to move.

The single word on the paper that now lay on the floor?

Publish.

A PRELIMINARY THOUGHT...

A friend stopped by as I was watering my backyard. There was a long narrow planting area along my woodshop. There were three hanging baskets of fuchsia.

"I noticed you water the baskets but not the ground cover..."

I nodded. "Yeah? So?"

"Don't you like the ground cover?"

I glanced his way as I carefully moved the watering can to the next hanging basket. "It's called Pope's spotted spurge."

His protest was almost whiny. "But you don't water it."

I looked over my sunglasses at him. "It's a weed."

"Then why have it?"

I returned to the water just starting to dribble from the bottom of the basket of fuchsias. "Because I'm a writer."

The look on his face was blank, misunderstanding.

I sighed. "It's like a character I might name after my ex or someone I hated in school growing up. They become a throwaway character. I take pleasure in killing them in horrible ways. It's their lot in life."

I reached down and demonstrated. Quickly, I pulled large handfuls of green plants out by the roots. They lay on the patio limp and impotent. With tomorrow's heat, they will cook-off to a brown char. By Saturday, they will be compost dust.

He stood limp, trying to get his mind around my weed patch and the characters in a book.

"You mean you make up characters—only to kill them?"

I moved to the next basket. "Would you prefer I drag Palin or Kissinger into my books?"

He probed at the dead weeds with his foot as he muttered, "They're dead."

"Palin is still somewhere—probably watching Putin, and the Kiss just had heart surgery at ninety-one…"

"No.... the plants."

I put down the empty watering can. "I need to go write now."

He toed at the weeds once more. "Okay." As he walked out of the gate, he took one more look at the weeds.

"I can box those up for you to take home if you want..."

He thought for a moment and gently shook his head as he walked down the driveway.

I wasn't sure if he would ever understand.

His name is okay… but maybe if I just change his hair color…

And *this*, people, is why I write.

1

BUILDING A WRITER

If you are going to be mischievous enough to get thrown out of a restaurant with a friend, you can't do any better than Jonathan Winters in a little diner named Patty's in Toluca Lake. Although riding nickel rides with Pam and Mark in a Chuckie Cheese in Mira Mesa is a close second. It's not always the company, and it's not always the restaurant—or in Jonathan's case, Hugh's Market at three in the morning. Valerie Perrine was just an innocent bystander holding a banana gun and a pineapple wanting to be a grenade. It would have been a classic fruit salad... but alas... we'll always have aisle three.

Of course, nobody starts living in their twenties. The big stuff is already prepared by all the little trials that occur before. There are thousands of tiny bits and pieces one needs to sew together before the being, which, in my case, some days, can be mistaken for Frankenstein's creation.

My loving wife often refers to me as Mr. Zipper. But then, she's only been around for twenty-nine of the now sixty surgeries.

Colleges and universities and other Ponzi schemes would like you to believe they can teach you how to be a writer. I can show you how to drive a taxi, but I can't turn you into a cabbie. Writers and cabbies are created, not trained.

And before I start getting nasty mail, most editors are trained, but not actual storytellers. If Hemingway had a Chicago Manual of Style, it was probably a handy doorstop—or something for the forty-seven cats to use as a scratching pad or some other kind of padding for relief…

When I was two, I laughed so hard I threw up my hands in glee. The highchair tipped over. And my collarbone broke when my shoulder hit the sturdy coffee table. The table was a three-inch-thick slab of redwood supported by stout, ax-carved legs. It didn't budge—but my bone did.

The upper-body cast was put on, and the rail braces to bring my toes to point almost forward came off. Ever since then, I have walked like a duck with flat feet. At two, the good news is you don't remember things. But falling backward is a fear that haunts me to this day. Fear of falling at all would come later.

My father was a forest ranger. Growing up in a pine log cabin with the smell of chinking oakum are fuzzy memories—but vivid smell association. Okay, maybe just a disturbing penchant for the scent of pine and oakum. We lived in a tiny company logging town named Johnsondale. It was the last of the company-owned towns in California. The image on the cover of my book, *What About Marsha?*, is Johnsondale. There is no grittier growing-up than doing so in a logging or mining town.

In logging terminology, when the company owns the town, the mill, and everyone works for the company except the US postal lady, it is called a *show*. Johnsondale was a noticeably big show. About a hundred people worked at the lumber mill, with another hundred in the forest. There were nearly as many small white houses in three rows.

I DRINK COFFEE AND MAKE SHIT UP

For entertainment one summer (I assume it was the Fourth of July), many of the loggers and my father went to attack a giant log—felled decades before. The large boring ants had gotten to parts of it before it dried and hardened, so it had no lumber value. The men set to work with their chainsaws and two-man misery whips. The whips you usually see pictures of are the small six- or eight-foot saws with large teeth and a single man at one end. In any given logging camp, there were two-man whips—coming by their name with a cause. These are the great saws you only see in brown photos. They could stretch up to twenty feet in length for the big trees like the Sequoias and Redwoods.

I'm sure the day was a lot of fun, as the men and their families came away with many slabs for rough cut coffee tables. My mother changed my one brother and me on a slab table. I hold no grudge against the thing. A lifetime later, it is still in one of our family's homes.

I mention the coffee table, not because of my first broken bone, but because one of my first memories surrounds it.

Loggers wear special boots. They are called *corks*. A perfect description would be to think of combat boots with golf spikes. Many golf spikes. They are about a half-inch long and damned sharp. They are specifically sharp enough so when the logger is walking along a tree, the spikes or *tips* would entirely bury into the bark—thus preventing any kind of slipping. Now you know why those guys don't slip off during a log rolling contest. Don't try it with running shoes—they will just laugh at you while they take your money. They are standing on the reason you lost.

If there was a mat of any kind in their truck, it didn't last long. When they got dressed in the morning, it was with their corks on. When they had to go to the commissary, post office, or the company office, you guessed it—they had their corks on.

Every one's floors were made from pine. Every floor had dark dots where the Johnson floor wax filled in with each application. My mother hated those marks—and the men who didn't think twice about walking across a floor their "little woman" had slaved waxing all afternoon. They just wanted to know how soon dinner was.

One of those men, and I think I know which one, crossed corks with my mother.

My father never owned a pair. As the ranger, he wore more of a work hiking boot with a dense lug pattern. The lugs were much better in the mud, snow, forest floor duff, and floors. He also slipped them off at the door and padded around in his socks just as we kids did.

My memory was only a snapshot of the bottom of the corks, buried into the side of the slab coffee table just as if it was still a tree. It was very agitating.

Many years later, my mother remembered the evening as we were printing Christmas cards on our Kelsey press. Once she started telling the results of the set of corks in the side of her coffee table, we had to stop working—we were laughing almost too hard to even be standing up. (I'll talk more about those evenings later.)

The logger had come to talk with the ranger. My mother had been in the kitchen and hadn't monitored who came in or even thought about the corks. She was a little tired from herding us four children around all day as she stripped and re-waxed all the floors in the small cabin.

As the men sat down on the couch to go over some maps of the new logging area, the logger had absentmindedly relaxed and buried his corks, up to the leather soles, into my mother's prize possession. But not before he had stippled his way across the mirror of the freshly waxed floor. My mother came out of the kitchen with two fresh coffees. One she placed quietly on the coffee table. The other she quietly threw on the logger's chest and lap. Then, in an even tone, she instructed him to remove his corks and not to put them on until he got home and apologized to his wife.

Fifteen minutes later, he returned, still barefooted—in the snow. His wife's hand was attached to his twisted ear the entire time he apologized to my mother. After, his wife led them back to his truck.

Word gets around fast in a small town. By lunch, all the loggers knew not to wear their corks in the ranger's wife's cabin. By dinner time, they all knew they would never be welcome to wear their corks in any house. By Saturday, they knew they needed only to wear their corks in the forest or the mill—but don't go into the office.

The image of the bottom of his boot buried in the coffee table may not appear in any of my other books, but it is there as fodder. I was three at the time. What does appear as a theme, which seems to be pervasive in my books, would be strong women. Between my mother, Peg Mullen, Betty Denton, Dolly Welch, and Ms. Bemis, I didn't have a choice—I grew up with strong female role models.

Later in life, I wore corks for a brief time and hated them. I didn't regret throwing them away after they saved my toes, but the chainsaw did create quite a nasty trench type hole in the left cork. And whatever you have heard or thought about steel-toed boots... *forgetaboutit*.

The chainsaw was possessed—I'm sure about it. It later slapped sideways in a way where the breaker-bar (supposed to stop the chain) didn't. The flat blade hit my wrist and rapidly walked its way up my left arm until it had finally ground enough meat to bury the bite-teeth into the outside of my bicep. I used to think it hurt. But the surgeon working more than a few times on my right arm and shoulder convinced me the chainsaw damage was only a scratch.

Someday, at the risk of being accused of watching the *Chainsaw Massacre* too many times, I might use a logger to do some killing. Maybe Stihl chainsaws will pay me to use someone else's saw… But I'm also sure the logger must be wearing corks—

with three-inch-long spikes. You know—macho stuff. I wonder if Danny Trejo has ever done any logging?

A FINAL LESSON from the logging town—as you drive into the town of Johnsondale, the last I heard, there is a split of the street. The traffic goes around a huge stump the height of a two-story house... which is apropos—because there are two stories about the stump.

For years after we moved, we heard people still called the stump "Bill's Stump." If they still do, it's stupid. We moved from there over sixty years ago, and my father (Bill) died a couple of years ago—and the stump never grew there.

As I said, my father was the ranger. Most of his job was called "cruising timber." This means he walked up and down the mountains with two cans of spray paint in his pack—blue and orange—marking trees. The orange was sprayed in a large X, or a large X with a circle around it and slash through it. Both meant to cut the tree down. The circle and slash meant it wasn't good lumber material and to leave it downed where it falls. The log would become infested with boring beetles. Then bees would pollinate the returning growth, and finally, boring worms, ants, and termites providing food for bears, marmots, wolverines, skunks, lizards, and other things that create the diversity of a mature forest.

The blue paint was also displayed with a large X with a bar over and under. This designation was usually sprayed on deformed or otherwise physically damaged trees. The mark was to stop it from being harvested in a clear-cut or select-cut situation.

After the harvesting was done, a logger who knew how to set blasting charges and all, would shinny his way up to about thirty feet, and then wrap the tree in a loopy manner—with detonation cord. Then, as the logger—or powder monkey, as he is called—makes his way down and wraps each of the larger limbs with a half-hitch knot. The cord burns with a speed somewhere between the speed of sound and the speed of light.

A hundred feet of the line is almost an instantaneous explosion. The knots on the limbs blow the limbs off, either close to the trunk or will leave a tiny limb of one or two feet long. The loopy hanging of long loose loops in the middle of the tree provides for an explosion to shatter the top of the tree. These combinations of explosions turn the unusable standing tree into a large toothy standing snag that will die, become infested with bugs, which provide food for woodpeckers, which bore holes, which become homes for smaller birds. The shaggy, toothy top is a favorite for larger birds of prey. So the useless tree becomes an essential agent for the forest to become healthy while it grows back into a productive forest. Most of the bunny hugger people think an "old growth" forest is the best example of a forest—with its majestic trees towering overhead and creating a deep dark forest floor. They are wrong.

Large forest fires are the reset for just such stagnated monocultures that discourage the infestation of diversity in a forest. Deer will make their way through such a forest, but squirrels get nothing, and badgers hate the dark empty forest floor where brush and the healthy shrubs die from the lack of sunlight and oxygen exchange.

So back to the story of the stump…

Loggers look at trees with butts larger than thirty-inches thick and start drooling and hyperventilating. They may get a payday based on the days they work—but they also get board-bonuses for cutting trees with maximum net board footage. So, if a tree two loggers can't reach around and touch fingers gets their motors running—you can only imagine what a tree almost twelve feet thick would do to these guys. Let's just say it could give some loggers a woody so hard it would drive them blind.

In this tree's case—it had to have been a mass hysterical blindness.

My father had a large arm-swing when it came to marking timber. I've seen photos, and even in a grainy black and white, you could see his marks from a city block away. He also had a way of dotting the end of the second slash so he could tell if a logger had marked a rogue tree and cut it illegally—a terminal offense in a company show.

So, one fine day, my father was watching and checking the logs coming into the mill. When a truck came in carrying a single oversized log on his thirty-four-foot-long bed, the ranger took notice—he knew he had not cruised anything in the cut range larger than a six-foot butt. So there would always be at least three logs on a truck—not one single chunk of wood twelve feet across and thirty-six-feet long.

Note: In the 1950s, these were common sizes of trees. Today, a thirty-inch butt is a "fatty."

My father stopped the smiling trucker. He made the man get out of the truck, which made the trucker stop smiling. The ranger had sent a runner to get the yard boss. When the man arrived, my father pointed to the blue paint still in the cracks of the bark where it had not come off when the logger or loggers power scraped a chainsaw over the bark to remove the mark. The orange they left to forge a mark with hadn't been enough.

The yard boss looked at the massive trunk and commented at the board footage it could produce. The ranger laughed. He grabbed the long solid steel pinch bar used to tighten down the large chains holding the logs on the trailer. He held it over his head and down his back. And then took one giant chopping swing and banged the side of the large tree trunk. The deep hollow drum sounded through the yard. The tree was not solid—its center was rotten or hollow.

The yard boss stepped to the back and noted the logger's tags as to who had cut it. He turned to the trucker and told him to cut the gut wrappers (chains), and they pushed the log off the trailer where it was. The trucker was told to haul up—or square his debts and pay at the office—and then leave the mountain. He probably would have to sell his trailers and do some other kind of hauling—or go wildcat haul in Oregon or Washington. The loggers would be terminated later in the day. Their wives would be immediately told so they could start packing their possessions in preparation to vacate the company house in the evening. If they couldn't square their debt at the company store, they left with the shirts on their backs. The company was also the bank.

The yard boss had the trunk stood upright so it didn't take up so much space. It was also a sign all loggers and truckers would see as they came and went from the town. It was a constant reminder—what the ranger marks is the law.

As for lessons, one is about following rules. If you work for a company and take their pay, you follow their rules. If you don't like their rules, there is the road out of town. Don't hit the large stump.

The other lesson is about the name "Bill's Stump"—or even the title of the stump. The tree was high cut at about four feet off the ground. This makes it easier to handle the fifty-inch-long blades of the working saw. The double-ended chainsaws with an engine at both ends were always used above the beltline on a logger. So the log was never a stump.

Perception is a powerful thing. I used the lesson to a powerful conclusion in *Angel Flights*.

I'VE GOT to give my father one thing here with Johnsondale—he was industrious. In those days, a twelve-inch or fourteen-inch-thick log was considered a pecker-pole. It wasn't worth running through the mill because it would yield a pecker's worth of lumber. Most of these were the tops of trees, ranging eighty to well over a hundred feet tall.

My father would range out with a small hand saw and cut them to about eight feet long. After he got them home, he would split them into quarter-rails for a fence. There was about a half a mile of split-rail zig-zag fence around our yard. It was there for no better reason than to protect the two small noble fir trees from the roaming cattle. The one tree had connected to the ass-end of a cow who scratched until it cracked. The tree recovered, but with a crook in the trunk.

I only mention this fence because of two things. First, I know what kind of effort it takes to build so much fence as I built one. My property ran almost a half-mile along the road. I added some at both ends so it looked like it also ran back into the forest.

The second reason for mentioning my father's fence was the truck tire we kids had to play with. Now a zig-zag fence is just a stacked fence with no nails or fixtures to hold it together.

Once a large truck tire gets rolling down a hill, a stacked fence doesn't stand a chance. Something is going to give. I'm sure my father knew what kept blowing out the fence at the bottom of the small hill, but I don't remember any swats. But then, I was the sweet innocent golden child in diapers.

WHEN I WAS three and a half, we lived on the side of a highway. We kids could fall asleep counting cars as they passed us by on the two-lane road. The road ran from Placerville and Highway 50, up to Highway 80. Highway 80 is the northern pass route around Lake Tahoe—of the Donner Party fame. It was a long time between one and two cars, and even longer to get to a third car.

We only lived there for about nine months, but it was long enough to create many memories. The large pasteboard box on the front porch with clothes for dress-up created some lasting aftereffects. I'm sure running around with just a belt, an empty holster down the front, and the optional Tom Mix cowboy hat led to mixed feelings about being dressed or not.

I'm sure the mail lady who drove the brown truck got a kick out of the kid with nothing to hide but was well covered by the holster to past his knees. After that—and being on the receiving end of my "Indian" siblings the next summer—my aspirations of growing up to be a cowboy were... well, curbed.

WE HAD CHICKENS. If you have never opened a small door on a chicken coop, reached in under the warm body of a laying hen, and pulled out a warm egg—you just don't know what real living is.

There is something extraordinarily Zen about feeding birds running free. I'm not talking about bird feeders with seeds in a jar or suet apples hung in trees—we're talking sticking your hand down into a bucket of yeasty smelling cracked field corn and then casting it about on the ground and the backs of the bent-over chickens.

Sitting in a park throwing bits of bread or cracked sunflower seeds to pigeons is a very frail third place to casting corn to your chickens. Not that I would want to have chickens again...

The memories of a chicken with its head sticking out of a hole in a paper bag aren't quite as vivid as the headless body rustling the bag around the yard a moment later. We had chickens... until the temperature dipped so low one night the combined heat in the coup wasn't enough. We had chickens... in the freezer. We ate ground beef and pasta for the next month. Chicken just didn't seem appealing—to eat—or cook.

My father went away for a forest fire. He was gone more than a day or two. For me, this was something new. I think it was something new for him too. He had started his career on a forest lookout atop a mountain. Then he cruised timber in Johnsondale. Now he was fighting forest fires. This was the first time I consciously paid attention to him not being around much.

One afternoon, one of the green forest service trucks pulled slowly up our long driveway to the barnyard back area. The man, who lived "next door" (about a mile down the road) and had two or three kids our age, got out of the driver's side. And then a big roly-poly man got out of the other side. His clothes didn't fit. His shirt was wide open, and the big chest and belly protruded like a beach ball. The pants were tied on with some rope but still wide open with a gap of many inches. He was barefoot and stood on small hams sticking out of his skin-tight work pants, which were usually worn baggie.

We kids just stood with open mouths and yelled for our mom.

As the back screen-door snapped shut, Mom was looking at the two men. Only one she knew. She was trying to ignore the strange fat man like people driving past a wreck. "What can I do for you, Ted?"

Ted pointed at the fat man. "Ruth, inside this balloon-man is your skinny husband. Sorry I had to bring him home in such a condition."

The fire had gotten into a grove of poison oak covered with poison ivy. Dad was one of the three firefighters who had breathed in the smoke and blew up. It was one of the few times I ever saw my father take time off.

The workaholic gene isn't a gene to take lightly. If not treated correctly, it can cause strife, tension, and expensive vacations requiring no pen and paper, or any other implement of writing. But it can also produce a few books.

I DRINK COFFEE AND MAKE SHIT UP

The last memory of our time in Georgetown was a pit. The area wasn't big, even for a three-year-old. My guess would be in the neighborhood of only six or eight feet across, and about two or three feet deep. The entire hole was a mass of quartz crystals. Some the size of my small forearm, others were perfect tiny crystals smaller than the little pinky on my right foot. They ranged from crystal clear, to muddy white, to purple amethyst. There were so many perfect crystals—my mother's angst over only being able to keep six or eight haunted her for years. Years later, when I started hanging out with people into metaphysical woo-woo shit, I thought about how rich I could be if I could only find the hole again.

But—at three, I wondered if fairies came and took the crystals away to make windows or something. I think it was the start of creating stories. And now you know where a dragon blowing glass came from. She wasn't Norwegian at all—she came from a hole in the ground in Northern California.

By the time we moved to South Lake Tahoe, I was much more mature. I was almost four. This meant I was allowed out in the yard alone without one of the older siblings. This was as much of a blessing to them as it was to me. I just wanted to be left alone. They were thankful to be divested from the teat-suck of a younger pest.

The last time we kids did something "together" willingly was the rounds of mumps, followed immediately by the measles. By the end of those trying weeks of two bunk beds in a single room, we were all four ready to go back to school and go our own ways.

I'm sure when I get around to including a plague or something similar in a book, this experience will play a large part. I know being incarcerated in the tiny bedroom with my siblings played its role in the aftermaths ranging from torture, bullying to passive-aggressive paybacks. Nothing says love-hate like siblings.

As the youngest, there is usually the misconception we are the spoiled ones. I'm not here to deny there is some favoritism meted out, generally from the mother and rarely from the father. The paternal favoritism gets used up on the first, or at least the first son. What does get heaped on the youngest is shit. The adage about *shit rolls down hill* is true in families of more than one child. The second child may get a patch on the jeans, but the youngest is guaranteed at least one, and usually, there are two on the knees at a minimum. We won't even talk about underwear.

Summer was a great time to be a kid in Lake Tahoe. Davy Crocket had made his run but left a deep mark on the territory, or at least on us kids, and my mother. Mom cut all our hair. She had a professional set of clippers.

The day after school was out, the hair on both sides of our heads came off. Yup, we were rocking Mohawks before they were cool. I think if Mom could have gotten away with it—my sister would have been in the line-up as well.

As I look back, it must have been a vacation for my mother as well. She went the summer without having to cut most of our hair, except for me. Every week, I got mandatory white sidewalls. My middle brother went all summer and barely grew out what I put forth in a couple of weeks. It was the first of many such denigrations of fairness.

With the end of summer, we were back in the Saturday night routine of haircuts and baths. The 'hawks were sheared down to match the rest of the low-profile hair, usually barely over a boot camp cut of white sidewalls tapered into a #2 baby seal on top. For many years, our school pictures—which were typically taken the first month before shirts became torn and mended—showed us in military cuts. I'll explain about "sir" later.

We never got teased or taunted. I think the end of the 1950s was about "We're all dorks together." Maybe the dorkiness would explain why there was a lot more peace in the land.

Who cares? We were dorks and didn't know it or care. What I don't remember was any kids back then coming home with head lice. Evidently, lice don't like short hair, high altitude, or waiting for the school bus while the snowfall is enough to give you an *old man* look.

EVERYONE KNOWS that one child in a family will pound on or tease another sibling. It's almost expected.

Nobody expects the three older siblings to tie the squirt down almost naked on a red ant hill. Ah—the things kids learn by reading and watching bad westerns on Saturday morning television.

By the time one of the fire crew found me and untied me, I was the size of and shaped like my father was after he was exposed to the poison oak fire smoke. The fireman carried me to the ranger's house. Peg Mullen took one look at the splitting shorts and knew it wasn't one of her three little cherubs. The only other place with boys in it was ours.

The poor fire crewman presented me to Mom. "Is this one of yours? I found him staked out over a red ant nest." The red ants in Lake Tahoe are the larger kind—about the size of termites on steroids. Years later, I found out they were called fire ants. Go figure—they were on a forest service compound.

Mom turned around to the other three. When needed, she could growl. "You three are grounded. Go to the Mullen's until we get back." It was a fate worse than death—especially at lunchtime. Peg knew about peanut butter on white bread, but someone forgot to tell her you also need jam, so the mass doesn't stick to the roof of your mouth. She also had a thing for liverwurst.

The closest hospital at the time was in Reno, about two hours away. Mom called my father and explained the situation, threw me in the station wagon, and drove into the wind with me wearing my father's boxers and a holey T-shirt. I was dotted with angry red bite marks everywhere. Mom was sure I was going to split at the seams.

The professional school bus driver in her took over. She never panicked but maintained an urgent speed down the winding mountain grade into Nevada and Carson City. Knowing Mom, the needle on the speedometer was possibly two or three notches over the legal speed limit. She was no speed demon *in those days*. She was a school bus driver with the health and well-being of many children entrusted in her hands.

In Carson City, we had to stop at a red light. (I wrote about the light years later in *Light2Light*) She looked over to find the child she knew, swimming in his father's underwear. My swelling was all but gone. The angry red bites looked like last week's mosquito bites. I was a happy little boy on a big adventure with his mother… alone.

It was my first memory of being with my mother without the other three.

I remember my mother pulling to the side of the main street. Across the street was the museum we always liked to go through. It was free and ended with a walk through a "real" mine, and out through a turn-gate which faced a steam locomotive. It's still there for kids to climb on.

We went to the market where she bought me new shorts and a T-shirt. The reason I remember was that they were not hand-me-downs. They were mine and only mine. To this day, whenever I try on clothes, I mash the cloth up to my face, and smell the smell of new clothes, the feel of new clothes—and think of my mother looking down at me.

We went to lunch. I don't remember what we ate. I rarely do. But I remember the conversation was between just us. It was powerful and would influence the rest of my life. I'm not sure how a four-year-old's mind is supposed to work, but I did recognize I was finally alone with my mother—just me—no competition for conversation with older siblings. I also knew there was only one time during the day when she was alone—when she was setting type and printing. Those two activities are mind-numbing. They can be seen as either monotonous labor or a mind-soothing activity. I learned the latter through the years of evenings with my mother.

That day in the restaurant, Mom asked me what I wanted, really wanted. It was simple. I wanted to learn how to set the type she used to print things on her Kelsey printing press.

At age four, I started learning how to read—upside down and backward. Years later, it was still a joke with us. She would stand behind me and hug my shoulders as she asked if this was really what I wanted. Learning to set type had led to so much more. Reading at an early age led to us working up stories as we worked. It also led to some very real and sometimes brutally honest conversations.

I didn't learn, "See Dick run. Run, Dick, run." I learned things like "regional marine demolition and pier construction," or "ophthalmologist," which led to the understanding of the word "gynecologist" at the vaulted age of seven.

Every letter is pulled from a large tray and placed in the line on the small rack called a stick. Every word is upside down and backward. IF you want to know what it looks like—turn this book around 180-degrees. If you are reading this on an e-reader, you will need to stand on your head—or buy my paperback. No other book works quite like it.

This habit of reading upside down, as well as reading the books on the reachable shelves of our extensive family library, led to some remarkably interesting problems. First, every schoolteacher in the first four grades would call my mother, explaining they needed to have a little chat. Finally, when my fourth-grade teacher, Mr. Kaufman, made the concerned call about my strange way of reading—my mother cut him short.

"Is this about him reading with the book upside down?"

"Yes, well… um… there have been some recent breakthroughs about understanding reading disabilities which have con—"

My mother was sweet. Kind of like a fireball jawbreaker. "Before I take time off from *my* job, and you waste *my* time—ask him what he is reading—just for fun."

I thought it was a strange question coming from a teacher, who, on most days, acted as if he would rather we students disappear and leave him to his silent world he had problems staying out of. The bottle in his bottom drawer probably didn't help. It is funny how the kids know, and the adults ignore…

I explained I was reading the annotated version of Mary Shelly's *Frankenstein*—but was finding the scholarly dissections almost as impressive as the affected writing from a hundred years before. He didn't call my mother anymore. I was *not* scheduled for any more reading groups. It was just as well. I think they were reading *Tom Sawyer* at the time. I had covered him, Huck Finn, and parts of Twain's travels in the west, by the third grade.

I read books upside down until the seventh grade. Then I started to notice girls read their books right-side up.

Later, in my twenties, while in college, I would be diagnosed with mild dyslexia. But, by then, who cares. I was back up to reading over two thousand words a minute.

It seems like a quirky personal thing to write about, but then, this book is about the things in my life that make me the writer I am. Hemingway, Asimov, Louis L'Amour, and Victor Hugo have positively influenced my storytelling, but it was my quirky growing up that has set the tone of my stories.

My dyslexia and having read differently than others, I think, started me paying attention to quirks in others. Occasionally scattered in my books are mentally challenged, physically challenged, altered abilities, and physical deformities along with various skin colors, nationalities, sexes, and sexual preferences. They are there because they have always been in my world—deaf, blind, harelipped, clubbed foot, rickets, polio, cerebral palsy, LGBTQ+ of every cross-section, and more than my fair share of psychopathic friends—and family.

If the person seems so real that you might know them, it's probably because I did.

The dynamics of four kids in government housing can cause a lot of things. Bonding is not one of those. Well, not while the incarceration is in place.

My middle brother beat on me incessantly. Yeah, we are two years apart. So what else is new? My oldest brother generally didn't know or care if we existed. Sorry, I've got nothing new there either. The two of them shared one of the three bedrooms. My sister was locked away with the brat, so we fought like cats and dogs. Big sisters can hit harder, but they don't always win.

Being a devious creepy little brother, I would steal a pair of her panties and hide them down at the bottom of my bed where my smelly feet were. Mom would find it when she changed the sheets. At first, she thought I might be weird. Then, when she figured it out, she asked me to stop it and just get along with my sister instead of tormenting her. Yeah... like that worked...

My sister thought it was the yuckiest thing... and would have to be desperate to wear the affected pair again. She kept them piled on the left. That made it easier for me. I always took a fresh one from the right. Man, I was evil. But eventually, she got me back.

Childhood fights come in all shapes, sizes, and colors—not just black and blue but also red and yellow.

The folks were gone for the day—which was the first mistake. It was summer—the second mistake. There was nobody in charge… unless you count my useless dickwad of my oldest brother. This would qualify for mistakes numbering from three to five—as in, five o'clock when the folks got home.

I don't think any of us could tell you how it started, but we do know it began with the ketchup being in a squeeze bottle. So was the mustard. The honey was too—but it didn't work as well. But the homemade syrup worked simply fine, and luckily, the war *was* confined, for the most part, to the kitchen.

Someone was making something, and as usual, most of the upper cupboards were open to get food or maybe even a plate… instead of standing and eating over the sink as my father did.

I'm sure the fight lasted only a couple of minutes. But the cleanup took all the towels and a lot longer. The towels and rags got rinsed and used and finally thrown into the washing machine. Notice, I didn't say… "and washed."

We were enormously proud of our cover up. The kitchen sparkled—it was almost too clean.

The folks came home. Mom started banging around in the kitchen, making dinner. She spilled something and reached for a towel…

She started the clothes washer, which seemed to be full, and went to get a hand towel from the bathroom. Those had been used too, as had the face clothes. And a few bath towels. She grabbed one of my father's green forest service undershirts.

As she was just finishing cooking dinner, she went to set the plates out. She opened the cupboard to see a Michael Pollack painting in red, yellow, and syrup. As she stood there trying to figure out what she was looking at, a large dollop of red and yellow let go from the ceiling and landed on her nose and glasses.

Out came the belt, and then we were sent to bed. In the morning, we were laid to work cleaning everything before we got breakfast.

I'm sure we were grounded for a while as well. There is no warfare like family warfare.

SPEAKING of childhood punishment and my dickwad oldest brother, for a guy who could whip his superstar uncle at chess (while reading a science fiction book—or worse—a comic) and tested out in the genius range—he was sure stupid sometimes.

Now, I'm not saying he was selfish or a pig… or is it a hog? I'm just relating events. When it came to placing his favorite food on the table, he would always set the largest portion at his place, even if he were told it was for our father. Mom would switch it before we sat. His face always got dark as he screwed it into a tizzy-fit he didn't dare let out.

One day, his greed got the best of him.

We lived on a five-acre compound ringed by a large log fence. We were not allowed to "cross the fence" without permission. One day, someone from the ranger station had seen us not only past the fence but also across the highway.

My brother was in his bedroom reading and only heard the part where my father told the other three of us that we were "Going to get…"

That's when he was making too much noise jumping off his bed and running down the hall, yelling, "I get the biggest…"

I don't remember if our father could whip us while he was laughing or not. I don't remember if it spared us the whipping.

What I did learn was not hearing all the contents or conditions before you stake a claim—can make for an interesting outcome.

My middle brother is an excellent example of unexpected outcomes. My sister told him to wait at the bottom of the grease rack while she rode the toboggan down the snow on the rack. He sat near the end. Exactly right—so the side of his head was where the curve of the toboggan and its metal edge could hit him. Scar #1.

"Lay there and sight my croquette mallet and make sure I've got it lined up." Scar #2. He was now oh-for-two against my sister.

Fourth of July and a city fire truck came down the highway. The siren was always something to get our attention. The lights were just an added attraction. It turned into the housing development just past the forest service compound, and on the other side of the fence. The ten-year-old was off like a crazed antelope and twice as fast. He was bound and determined he would see where the fire was.

A few minutes later, he came back with a torn shirt and a four-inch gaping wound on his chest.

Barbecue was over, and it was off to the doctor for stitches. Running into a barbed wire fence can be a hard lesson… or give you fodder for a great lie later.

At fifteen, my brother David looked exactly like Michelangelo's statue by the same name. With oversized webbed feet, he swam for nothing but blue ribbons. Scar #3—which had become a keloid and much lighter than his seemingly perpetual tanned skin, to this day—had taken on a life of its own, and the other kids were impressed.

At one of the swimming meets, as he took yet another

ribbon, one of the other moms turned to my mother. "Your son is absolutely amazing."

"Thank you."

"No, really. It is amazing how far he can swim underwater and stuff with only the one lung."

"One lung?"

"Yes, you know—the scar where they removed his right lung."

I'm relatively sure he was too old to get the belt or be grounded by then, but I'm confident he got one of "Mom's little talks."

Years later, I got to steal the same story on my honeymoon. But my scars are much larger and more dramatic. I told the diving master it wasn't so hard when they took out the right lung… but then, holding up my left arm, I said it only got tough to breathe when they took out the left lung, as well. For some reason, he wouldn't let me dive anymore.

School has its moments, but sometimes the strong memories are carved into our souls by the coming and going to school. Riding a rural school bus is like no other experience. You either have a memorable bus driver, or you didn't. Only three stand out in my mind. The first was a huge cowboy of a man. The only thing missing on this Andy Devine knock-off was the hat and whiney voice. Everything else was there, from the boots to the huge belly shelved out over the large buckle.

As we got on the bus, his voice was soft enough to miss as his only greeting was, "Welcome, welcome." Chet had the verbal repertoire of a parakeet.

The man put up with a lot of rowdy kids, not like today's kids, where they are on the verge of getting locked up in Guantanamo, but rowdy in our own way. Mostly talk along with the occasional paper airplane.

One day, as the excitement of summer nearing, the noise level was at a breaking point.

Big Chet pulled the bus over to the side of the highway. He set the brake and turned the bus off. He stood up—all forty-seven feet of him. He glared down the length of the thirty-eight children and hiked up his belt and pants. There was dead silence. None of us had ever seen the man standing. A ten-gallon hat would have been crushed against the ceiling. (My mother, also a driver, years later told me he stood just over six and a half feet tall. He was indeed a mountain of a man.)

He quietly splayed his hands out over his hips as he slowly made eye contact with every single kid. Finally, he eased out in a quiet yet penetrating deep booming voice, "I've just about had my belly full." We all looked at the single button straining to keep it all in.

He turned and opened the doors. Thirty-eight sets of eyes followed him as he casually walked down the stairs and stepped off the bus. He sauntered to the back of the bus and about twenty feet beyond. Only those of us near the back open windows could hear—as he spoke more than twenty words to the forest behind us.

He took in a few large breaths as we watched his huge shoulders swell and sag.

He returned. Started the engine. Stared in the mirror for a minute. Closed the door and drove the rest of the delivery route in dead silence.

During the few weeks remaining, we kids spoke only in soft voices. There was no horseplay.

On the last day of school, Chet watched as each child in his care departed and softly spoke, "Have a great summer, and I'll see you next fall."

He never did. During the summer, he died of a heart attack.

The man left his legacy in my mind. He was a gentle giant of a man who only once told kids he had a belly full. If my brother David reads this, I know he will softly laugh. Chet was some kind of memorable.

THE SECOND DRIVER was only memorable for driving a small bus and taught us five children our first dirty limerick. Claim to fame —and gone by Easter.

THE THIRD DRIVER was my own mother—but as I found at my fortieth high school reunion—she had been like a second mother to so many others. One former student sat me down—thirty years had passed since my mother died—and she was still taking it hard. Her own parents had passed, but their passing hadn't fazed her as much. We held each other and cried for a long time. She reminded me of the day Mom had stopped the bus and talked to all of us kids.

So those of you who never road a bus, or at least a rural bus, will understand the impact of stopping a bus. Making stops is something they do. Turning the bus off is only something they do when the driver needs to walk a child across the highway. These days they have a long arm with a stop sign on it, which swings out from the bus. The flashing red lights and those signs haven't saved a tenth of the kids a live bus driver ever did.

No, what we are talking about here is a driver pulling over to the side of the road and turning off the engine.

First, the bus is never to leave the travel lane. It is the big visual wall there to protect kids. Second, the engine is to be left running unless the driver is leaving the bus.

When a driver eases over to the side of the road, parks, sets the break, and turns off the motor—it gets a kid's attention. To ignore those signs of pending importance is to be some special kind of stupid.

As kids were, are, and always will be—we could be cruel in those little ways. Unbidden nicknames, not sitting next to someone—and making a big point about it. And, of course, there is the out-right picking on someone or blatant bullying. Mom, Mrs. Charlton, the bus driver—saw it all. She knew every name. Bishop was and still is a small town—Mom knew everyone's parents. She was also a medical transcriber at the hospital, Girl Scout leader, community art council director, and some zillion other things that turn a small town into a thriving community. She knew everyone—inside and out.

As each child got on the bus every morning and every afternoon, she called them by name and asked them something about their day—every kid. Every single child on her bus route knew every day, twice a day, Mrs. Charlton made sure they were alive and okay. It was just one of those little things Mrs. Charlton did…

I wouldn't tell you even if I could remember who it was getting picked on the day she stopped the bus. The bus was never loud. Most of us kids were just numbly sitting—staring out of the windows—recovering from the day.

Suddenly, Mom was pulling the bus over right in the middle of the Indian reservation. *There were no stops here*. The bus went silent. Mom sat in her seat, staring up into the huge mirror above her head. She was not a large woman. Her head barely floated above the seat of the biggest school bus they made. At the time, she was the only woman who had ever passed the Crown 77 driving test. Now she sat quietly watching. Her left hand moved, and the air brakes engaged, and then to reinforce the quiet—she turned the motor off. After a moment, she stood up.

She leaned her hip against the pole. Every child in her care was on the bus. Every child could feel those special eyes—upon them. Every child—waited.

"Suppose… for just a moment… fairy tale characters are real." She was quiet, but every child could hear her. Only I knew this side of my mother—the one who saw things—differently.

"Suppose… those characters in all the nursery rhymes and fairy tales had to live somewhere. Suppose, between the telling of their stories, they had to go to work—to live real lives and make a living. They pay taxes, buy food, see the doctor, just like you, me, and your parents."

Mom pointed toward one of the boys. "Who was at the top of the beanstalk?"

"Umm… the giant…?"

She turned to the other side of the bus. "Who knows the locksmith in town?"

All the hands went up. Everyone knew H. O. "Tiny" Robinson. The man was hard to miss. He stood almost six and a half feet tall and weighed slightly over four hundred pounds. The Ford Econoline Van he drove was permanently slouched down on only the driver's side. What most people didn't know—except for the women in town who liked to dance—was the man's idols were Fred Astaire and Gene Kelly. The man was probably the only male in our mule town who owned a legitimate pair of dancing slippers. Any woman in Bishop, who danced, would jump at the chance to take a whirl around the floor with Tiny.

"What about Jiminy Cricket?" We all thought it until someone called out the name.

"Snow White? Red Riding Hood… The flower seller… Mother Hubbard… Chicken Little…" and the names went on—and the answers responded.

Finally, she held up her one index finger… and she grew her special teaching smile. "You never know who someone really is. The person you are kind to, the person you ignore, the person you are less than kind to… You just never know." As she turned and sat down, she closed the door. "But…" Her eyes scanned the kids. "It does make you think…"

She started the bus, set the blinker, looked at the empty road in the mirror, and eased the big bus back on the highway.

Who could have known forty-some years later… there would be a show based on just such an idea? Bus drivers—some things just aren't what they seem. And, sometimes… you have to, or get to—share your mom.

"ONCE IN A BLUE MOON"—is a term referring to something happening, which is so rare, generations can come and go between events. The blue moon part came after two-thirds of the island of Krakatoa (a volcano) disappeared in a series of violent eruptions in 1883. The explosion was so violent and forceful that the ash was thrown into the upper atmosphere where it remained for years. The light-filtering nature of the ash created a color-shift that left the moon colored blue instead of white. The ash in the upper atmosphere was so dense—it spread around the world and from pole to pole. The phenomenon of the Blue Moon was recorded in cities as far north as Oslo and as far south as Durbin, South Africa.

And why do I mention this term? Because there is a similar phenomenon that happens only when there is just enough volcanic ash in the stratosphere, the moon is full. The temperature is between minus ten and twenty degrees, which has stopped the fall of snow. The last snow to fall is the magical coat. The crystalline structure is more of a horror frost than the open lace of snow. The event creates what is known as "Blue Snow." The color of the fresh snow is somewhere between an electric cornflower and a neon light blue.

The winter of 1957-1958 was the winter Mom and my father bundled us up in our blankets and carried us out to see not only a

Blue Snow but also several nights of intense Aurora Borealis along with the tiny scintillating dot in the night sky of Sputnik passing overhead.

Someone asked me why I never minded working on holidays. I guess you would have to have good memories of things—to want to recapture those moments. Vacationing is the same.

The "Family Vacation" came in 1959. My father had spent some time having a supercharger installed in the Studebaker wagon. We lived at 8,000-foot elevation, and we would be driving to the California coast. Somewhere along the line, he had become convinced the "mountain" car would need help with the thicker air of the lower elevation. I only mention this because I remember the weekend of the car's hood up, my mechanically ignorant father staring blankly at the mystical mechanical wizardry, and the hands of the forest service mule skinner installing the supercharger.

The dichotomy wasn't lost on me. It later forced me to learn and understand the engines I could and know when to leave the others to the experts. The comedy of the Studebaker in 1959, and the large puddle of black motor oil on the hardwood floor of my second-story apartment in 1972—where I learned about VW engines and the value of planning ahead—led to a forty-year friendship and some strong characters in one of my crime series.

The "Family Vacation" was the only one we did as all six of us. We saw the obligatory people and came home. Other families would go visit an uncle and family for a few days so the kids could get a feel for their cousins. We got five to six hours. It would be up to us as adults to reach out and get to know, or not know, our extended families.

At the time, there were thirteen Charlton families in the Riverside, California, phone book. We were related to twelve of those. We children were told not to ask about the "other" name. Years later, my favorite great aunt shared much of what the rest of the family wanted to stay hidden. She confided about the "other" family being colored. Which, I guess, was a real mystery for the other twelve—being the White Anglo-Saxon Protestant immigrants from England they were.

At the time, and until I was about sixteen, I had never cognitively met a "person of color." The mountains of California were pretty much homogeneously without distinction in my mind. This is not to say they were all white. There were plenty of "others" in my life purview, but nothing made them stand out as "different."

In Johnsondale, we had a babysitter or nanny who was the young daughter of the only logger of color. Which would mean the swarthy loggers of Greek, Irish, or Slavic descent weren't seen as different. I would assume the men or families from Latin America, the First Nation, or anyone else not readily identified, were also lumped into the pejorative term of just being a logger and below our notice.

Bennie was the produce department head at Ink's Market at the "Y" of South Lake Tahoe. I believe he was either Chinese or Filipino. His wife was Filipino and taught my mother how to make homemade tortillas. But I will be forever thankful for Bennie giving my mother some cookbooks. The first was Chinese food, and the second came a year later and was Japanese. I have held every restaurant to Mom's high standard ever since. Few have mastered Suki Yaki (pronounced Ski-yauki) like my mother did. Cuban Hash or Picadillo Crello came later.

So you might be scratching your head here. What does going on vacation, meeting people of different races and national heritage, and food have in common? They may not have been on my father's agenda, but they now rank up near the top of mine.

I get accused of writing my books between meals. As one of my editors put it—my characters eat a lot and then wash it all down with lots of coffee. It would take her a few years to mention my unabashed airing of the morning throne. I make no apologies. The first thing you did this morning was head for the toilet.

As for the food and drink, it has always amazed me how a character can go for two hundred minutes on screen and never sleep, eat, or drink anything. (Hint: I'll cover this in greater detail in another chapter.)

Toilet scenes are still relegated to the morning mirror soliloquies.

Then, there is the opposite in story writing. It is fondly referred to as "the campfire." You will see it in almost every movie, and now, you will never miss it when it happens.

The action of the story is moving along. Maybe there was a shootout, or a car chase, or just something emotional. Either way, the tempo needs to be slowed down, and there needs to be some explaining about what is motivating the lead actors to do what they are doing. Sometimes, it's the backstory. Sometimes, it's just what they have been trying to work out in their heads. Either way, there needs to be a reason for two or more characters to sit and talk—explaining to the audience what is going on.

In real life, we call this the family dinner, or a dinner date, or meeting the gang at the bar for a few drinks and some darts. Most people eat at least a couple of times a day. Many people drink coffee. If you don't like what I'm serving for the meal, go make your own campfire.

As in *Angel Flights*, it is critical to the story that Gabe be at the Dos Palmas Café and meets Zorro's niece and nephew. There is also a whole chapter, which is nothing more than a love story. Early into editing, my first editor was concerned about the word length of the book—it was long, dense, and weighty. Her comment was for me to "delete the chapter, and the story wouldn't suffer a whit." I told her we would revisit the subject after she was finished with round one of the editing. Those who read the book will know which chapter is still there.

Nothing I write is a throwaway... unless the guy in the red shirt doesn't get introduced.

While I'm talking about Mom cooking the world—there wasn't an ethnic recipe she didn't love and had worked hard to master.

I know, or recognize, my name—or at least the word for the animal bear—in about twenty or so languages. It is one of the reasons I, as well as others, love my name. The effort of having learned how to say hello in several languages—I lay at my mother's feet. And I silently thank her every time I eat in an ethnic restaurant and greet them in a language other than English.

I don't remember what started the conversation, but we got around to immigrants. My father was born in Canada to English parents who were on their way to become American citizens. Dad came down at age three. On my mother's side, the bloodline landed on the Mayflower.

The upshot of the conversation was Mom explaining, (in those days) a quarter of a million people, every year—gathered their belongings into a single bag, suitcase, or trunk, said goodbye for the last time to their home, their family, and their country, and moved to America. Once here, they learn one of the most difficult languages, learn about our history, and learn how our society works. Maybe they learn how to drive—and some learn enough to open a small business or restaurant. They have given up *everything* to provide me with a great place to eat, other than a burger, steak, or pizza.

The least I could do was to learn how to greet them in their native language, and hopefully—to also learn how to say please and thank you.

Mom was always Mom.

I DRINK COFFEE AND MAKE SHIT UP

The winter of 1959 was the year we went to bed with four feet of snow on the ground and woke-up with the houses buried. We had to dig tunnels to get out.

My father would fill the utility sink full of packed snow, and Mom would pour boiling water on it to melt it. It was a long and painful process. Time was of the essence as the snow was wet and heavy and needed to be removed from the roofs of the older barracks and homes.

The men had long rods that screwed together. They were war surplus antennas off Army tanks—they were used to probe for bodies after an avalanche. They used them to probe for the edges of the buildings.

One energetic young ranger was going to town shoveling snow—until the probe sunk about twelve feet behind him. One of the men laughed and told him he didn't need to worry about digging out the swing set just yet.

Some of the walkways, from building to building, on the forest service compound, became tunnels people could just ski over. I don't remember how long the walks remained walled with twelve to sixteen feet of snow, but I do remember we kids got in trouble for jumping off the gable of the house into the snow in the yard—which was only ten feet below.

Cold country can leave a mark on people. For me, as a child who sleep-walked, the mark still invades my life to this day.

There were no locks on any of the houses on the forest service compound. Not even little latches from the inside. The biggest fear for a ranger is to be trapped in a burning house. So for a kid of four or so years old, who loved to "go out and play in the sunshine," it was nothing just to open the door and walk out.

(Unless you're snowed in. Then you leave a body shaped dent in the wall of snow.)

Mother was psychic. Some would call it mother's intuition, but hers was beyond anything mild.

When she and Dad were dating, and he would be coming back into town unannounced, he would look at his watch as he hit the city limits in the middle of the night. In the morning, she would tell him when she awoke in the middle of the night and looked at the clock. Mom was psychic.

Mom's biggest fear in those days of my sleepwalking was she would sleep through her alarm, telling her one of the kids was missing. Over time, those ten and fifteen minutes, naked in the snow, took their toll. I have less than thirty percent feeling in my legs. Walking like Frankenstein, or stiffly, is an easy vision to conger up in a story. The colloquialism I like most comes from the Wild West I grew up in. Old broken-down cowboys walk all stoved up like they were walking with their legs in stovepipes.

Yup... cold country can certainly leave its mark on a person. These days, I love shoveling the rain.

The last day in Lake Tahoe, I spent a bit of time "in" Lake Tahoe. I was nine and was probably considered a potential risk to have around as the movers boxed up and loaded all in the moving van. So I was shipped off.

Friends of my parents owned a company that took out old docks and installed new ones. Pat, the owner, had two old military landing craft called Ducks. They could drive down the highway and then drive right out into the water and be used as workboats. I was the envy of my siblings as my Duck limo showed up in the morning to take me to work.

My day was spent riding around in and out of the lake on the Duck as we tended to the construction being done with the large crane on a barge. I remember the dark green glasses Pat gave me to protect my eyes from becoming sunburned on the water. (They are the same glasses Thorny Wallace wears in *Death in the Valley*.)

At the end of the workday, a few of the men and I stripped down to just our underwear (if we wore any) and went swimming to rinse the day's work off. I probably only imagined I had gotten as sweaty as the men, but who cares; we were having fun. I don't think we could get away with any such Tom Sawyer-ism today.

But including a kid in the fun after hanging out on a worksite all day should always be favored.

BISHOP WAS AN AMAZING PLACE, starting with arriving shortly after midnight. We drove down real city streets with row after row of meticulously kept houses. And for the first time in my life, sidewalks, not mud tracks passing as flat roadside, but honest to goodness concrete sidewalks.

The next surprise was stopping at a house, and the man who had the key mounted a bicycle leaning against the house. In shorts and a T-shirt, he rode through the streets to our new house. He didn't have a key, as there were no locks on any of the three doors, but he had rented the place for us, and so only he knew where it was. The fact of the house not having locks—wouldn't surprise me until years later.

The fact of living in a community with no locks on the doors struck me silly years later, but it also made it into *Stoneheart*.

Who would have guessed? Something as simple as a lock or no lock on doors could make such an impression on a mind. But different times and different circumstances are what creating a feeling in a book is about.

Eventually, my father had a lock installed on the front door. The side and back doors were lockless. The first house I rented myself was the same. You can read about the house and the lack of need for a lock on the back door in my *Angel Flights*. Nothing beats having a large guard snake, backed up by hot and cold running cops.

I REMEMBER the first day in Bishop. We had packed in the moving van all but two bicycles. Our father lent us his Timex watch. In teams of two, we ventured out. We had one hour—then had to return for the other two to have their turn. We started at six o'clock or shortly after sun-up. By ten o'clock, we knew the "city" had an Olympic sized pool at a *REAL* park. There was not only a Sears's catalog store but also a Monkey Wards and a JC Penny store. There was a Western Auto with new bicycles in the window and a real bookstore. At five minutes to ten, the four of us were sitting on the steps of the county library three blocks away from the house—to get our library cards.

The librarian walked up, saw us, and quipped. "Four children. You must be the Charlton children." It was as amazing as Mary Poppins was to her charges many years later. It took a while for us to find out about the three houses that shared our driveway and parking area. Mrs. Parent's house was the third one. She was our neighbor. Many years later, I would cross paths with her son, who was much older than us.

UNTIL I MOVED TO BISHOP, Mule Capital of the World, I had gotten into only one fight outside of my brother. He had been my best friend at school and in Cub Scouts. We had wondered what it was like to actually hit someone, not wrestle, but hit. Mrs. Cornick stopped us as we stood laughing and hitting each other's shoulders.

I DRINK COFFEE AND MAKE SHIT UP

As the new kid in town, I was ripe to be tried out by the town bullies. All of them were well versed in the use of fists, and not just on shoulders.

I won't dwell on this, but bullying is a very strange and pervasive, if not also perverse phenomenon. The first bloody nose came at the hands of the town ruffian. Shortly after, he was shipped off to juvenile hall or just moved. I didn't care which.

The next bully is the one I learned over many years about the dynamics of the beast. He was a smooth talker and came from a family with questionable favoritism. But through intimidation, he created a universe he could operate in. This early cooperation through deferred torment became my strongest learning experience about bullies. After all, I had been tormented by my middle brother for most of my life—this guy was just a little more painful.

I had made tentative friendships with a couple of other boys in my class. We were walking home, and one suggested a shortcut. The shortcut led to a small fenced-in parking area. The bully was waiting and laughing at my gullibility.

My lesson was never to trust those three guys again. In fact, it took years for me to realize that not everyone is a traitor or has a weakness of character. But also, the fuller you create characters to be human, attributes aren't black and white but more shades of gray.

About the time I was helping find people for my twenty-year reunion, I learned the last part of the bully. He had not grown up and learned magically how wrong bullying was. He had grown up enough to find out girls could be abused even worse. By the time we graduated from high school, he had one abortion and one child to his name—along with four other girls who had told him no, but he had had his way with them anyway.

I tracked him down and told him not to show up for the twentieth. I was not afraid to get up on stage and tell all. Luckily, he didn't. I don't think I would have. It would have just embarrassed the women who had moved on with their lives. One of them, years later, thanked me for letting it go—but also for having stood up to him and told him not to come.

I'm fine—now. But I'm also an author—revenge is mine thus sayeth the editor.

THE DYNAMICS of small towns in rural America are interesting. Some operate like a semi-dysfunctional family, and others operate under a patriarch—who is not always the mayor or kindly.

Then there are the blends. Bishop was such a hybrid. Sometimes the mayor was a figurehead. Other times, just a twit with friends. The real flow was, for the most part, controlled by a few old families, a few newer families, and all of them rich enough to believe they were owed control. The funniest part was the truly wealthy let them run around making noise until it was time to take them down a notch. Then the real power came out.

Such was the last whorehouse in town. The girls were clean, quiet, and respectful. The house was the second floor over the old police station. The madam was Big Bertha and a patron of the schools, parks, and anything else, making the town a great placed to live or grow up. The puritan wives of town—were not amused. They got on their high horses and told her to leave town.

Bertha was slow to anger. She loved Bishop. She knew everyone who was anyone. She told the ladies they most certainly did not want to do this.

They pushed—and finally demanded.

She acquiesced.

And the next week's newspaper, she bought the front page. She published her top hundred customers. Next to their names were listed what they liked, which girls they repeatedly asked for, how often they frequented her establishment, and how much they spent on the average year. Bertha also published a list of "gifts" and whom she had received them from. Many families left town, and some just dropped out of their churches.

The regrettable part of it all was the town lost one its true benefactors, cheerleaders, promoters, and an all-around nice person. I met her years later and found she still missed living in the community she loved. The small town of Laughlin, Nevada, was quiet, but not the same.

It was probably a regrettable fact also, her explanatory table of her top one hundred customers had left no room for the long list of good things she and her girls had provided for the community. How do you explain grass seed for the high school football and baseball fields, better lights for streets, land and backstops for baseball diamonds for the city park, or simple things like paper and pencils for the elementary school when a budget was pinched, and they ran out?

When First Lady Hilary Clinton spoke about it taking the whole village… she never used the words *but*, *except*, or *without*. A village, town, or city consists of everyone. Inclusive.

The lesson of Bertha always stuck with me—and it is a cornerstone in many of my writings. Role model women come in all shapes, sizes, and career paths. That brief time over coffee is the reason I brought her back to Bishop in my Thorny Wallace series.

YEARS LATER, the town got a taste of one of the other strong, quiet women in town.

I would have to place her as my second mother for the early years of my life in Bishop. She conducted a special tough love you really wanted. Betty was Betty, whether she was standing at her kitchen sink or helping while her husband sewed up the dog bite in my arm. Nothing ever waivered with her—she always had a clear view of what was right, and by God, it was going to be her way.

Bishop and its mayor were drifting. Things were just getting a little off track. Election year was upon us, and the mealy-mouthed mayor, seeking reelection, was addressing a crowded room at the PTA meeting. It was a repeat of two years before, which had been a repeat of the years before.

In the middle of his speech, Betty quietly stood up.

His speech corkscrewed into a few words of sputtering mumble. He acknowledged Betty.

In four short words, Betty put everyone on notice. *"I'm running for mayor."*

The current mayor knew instantly where his bread was and how it was buttered. He opened his mouth and said, "I'll be the first to vote for you." And then he quietly sat down.

The landslide was the closest to unanimous as it could have gotten. No other fool jumped in.

She cleaned up the town and then didn't run again.

I'd like to say Clint Eastwood and Carmel by the Sea learned from Betty, but he probably never paid much attention to Bishop. After all, horses are horses, and mules are mules. Bishop is the Mule Capital of the World, and the other city by the big water…

Bishop has had a lot of movies filmed there and around there over the years. If you ever watch any black and white cowboy movies about moving a lot of cattle—it wasn't filmed there—per se. But if there was a trail cook everyone called Cookie in the movie… we also knew him as Cookie—or Elisha Cook—long-time resident and all-around nice guy.

We had our share of big stars too. Steve McQueen jumped out

of the whorehouse window and had a knife fight at the corrals when they filmed *Nevada Smith*. The sets were built well and are still out there as part of the Laws Museum. Steve was well-liked. He liked the people in Bishop, and he liked staying at one of the smaller motels when they filmed there. He usually liked cabin five. It was closest to the lawn where others would have a noisy pool. He liked to read.

We had our snobs too.

Charlton Heston came to town to film *Will Penny*. Nice movie —but he was still a self-important jerk. About the second week into filming, Heston grumped at his usual seat at the counter of Jack's—one of the two 24-hour cafes. A good friend of Cookie's decided to have a little fun at Heston's expense. The conversation went something like this:

Crusty old-timer: "Hey, don't I know you?"

Heston: "I don't think so."

Crusty: "Yeah, yeah. I know this face." He moves a little closer so Heston can get the full olfactory effect of the cologne "eu de barnyard" and splashed-on four a.m. whiskey.

Heston gets it full bore and shudders: "Maybe you know me from your local movie house."

Crusty draws it out… Timing is everything: "Well… maybe… where do you sit?"

Don't mess with real country—you're gonna lose.

And if you are going to write about country—it ain't the same as rural. And for damn sure… don't write about it from the seventh floor of some fool-assed high-rise in Hollywood and expect it to sound like anything but horse shit. There is a big difference in smell, consistency, and usage between horse shit, bull shit, and mule shit.

My mother and I met Betty Denton and her husband, Dr. Bob Denton, a week or so after we moved to town. It was days before I started in the fifth grade.

A bunch of the kids from the neighborhood around the high school were playing tag under the huge elm trees canopying the city block of grass in front of the administration building. The grassy area was the town's second park. There was a wide sidewalk down the center, which was great for skating on, riding bikes on, and later for learning how to skateboard.

I was tagged as "It." I took off chasing the little girl. I never saw her family's protective Doberman pinscher.

I'm sure I had a stunned look on my face as I sat on the table in the small emergency operating room at the county hospital. Mom stood by the door. This was not the way either of us had expected things to start in the new town.

Fate—sometimes has other ideas.

The door whooshed with disturbed air as it swung open to a bustling man in a white coat. His hand was out as he rushed straight at me. Busy to get to the next hand to shake, next person to meet or talk to, and the next chance to laugh.

"Hi, my name is Bob Denton." His mustache did nothing to hide the scar on his lip. His nasal voice would have given him away anyway. It wouldn't have mattered. It never had—as I was soon to find out.

The tall, substantial nurse stood near the door, next to my mother.

"So... a dog bit ya, huh?" Bob was off and running with the cleaning. The best I could do was keep up with a nod of my head.

"Did you ever hear about the boy named Mark, who was always late for dinner?" He didn't even wait for the shake of my head.

"Well... he was always late. Finally, his dad said if he was late one more time—he would beat him until his bottom fell off."

I DRINK COFFEE AND MAKE SHIT UP

The doc probed around inside the bite after numbing it with lidocaine.

"So... one night, Mark knew he would be late—unless he took the shortcut." Bob's eyes got big. "Through the cemetery."

Mom looked with a question at the nurse. The nurse just slowly closed her eyes and rolled her head—nodding.

"So Mark starts walking across the big cemetery—but, out in the dark, he hears someone or something call his name. Mark. Mark." Bob tweezed open the wound and looked in with the same instrument doctors use in ears and noses.

"Mark took off running." He withdrew the instrument.

"He was scared. Whatever was calling his name was getting closer. Mark. Mark!" He pushed the curved needle into my arm and took the first stitch.

"He was running so fast—he never saw the new open grave. Wham!" He tied off the second stitch and snipped off the extra thread.

"There he lay... in the bottom of the grave... looking up. He just knew he was going to die." He held up the regular bandage and snarled at it—not a manly enough looking bandage for a manly wound. He pulled out the 4x4 square and started peeling off the tape.

"Suddenly—a big black dog came to the edge of the grave and looked down. Mark could see in the moonlight a big nasty hair-lip on the dog." Bob drew a jagged line with his index finger —dramatically up his face—from his mouth to his eye. "The dog looked down into the grave and barked—Mark! Mark, mark."

The bandage was done.

My mother was shocked. She turned to the nurse. Betty rolled her eyes. "This is what I have to live with." She stuck her hand out. "I'm Betty Denton, and you have completely met my husband, Bob. We have three children. My middle one, Billy, is about your son's age. Suzie is two years older, and Margie is three years younger. We live on Keogh Street. Just ask anyone where—

we have a recreation room with a pool table which is right next to the swimming pool. Your kids will probably be at our house." (We were.)

Bob turned to me and gave me one of my greatest life lessons. "So… you're all set. Now, I think I know all the hair-lip jokes out there—but just in case—if you hear any, you come tell me so I can make sure."

Don't hide what makes you different—celebrate it and make it your strength. It might just help someone else find theirs. (I couldn't let Bob or his lesson go. So I put him, harelip and all, in the second Thorny Wallace novel: *Light to Light*.)

As a side note: Everyone thought Billy would grow up and become the next Doctor Denton. He screwed around climbing mountains—and then found his muse in cooking. His studies in Paris left its mark on him—his French accent is as permanent as his father's upper lip and sense of life.

Margie, the Maggot, the Magattack, the Magnet… She became the current and third Dr. Denton in town—just like her grandfather and father before her. The town survived her dad's lip and sense of humor, her mother's term in office—I'm sure it will survive and embrace her charming smile and Tinker Bell laugh, as well.

I know I'm a better person for having been part of their family as well.

BEING AN EXTREMELY SHY KID, whose neighbor is the high school and the front yard is the school's front lawn, had its ramifications on my life education.

The first lesson came when we first moved there. My mother went into their bedroom one night, and just before she turned on the light, she saw red lights moving around on the lawn in front of our house. Now, just about anyone who lives or had lived in

I DRINK COFFEE AND MAKE SHIT UP

Bishop, and had even a distant connection to fishing, will now be laughing—and know exactly what we were about to find out.

The people crawling around in front of our house with red cellophane rubber-banded over their flashlight—were hunting for big fat nightcrawlers. The going rate Mac's Sporting Goods was paying in 1962—was two cents a worm.

At the sound of hard cash, I started crawling. It didn't take me long to have some serious change in my pocket to go to the Saturday matinée. Which—is where I learned another, more profound lesson.

The first lesson was with a little effort, small sums of money can be made—no matter who you are. Hunting worms, sweeping out a welding shop, running errands for shop owners stuck during lunch in a town with take-out—but no delivery. Even the shy kid found money with truly little asking.

The lesson at the matinée came the next summer. It has to do with the opposite of diabetes—it is low blood sugar or hypoglycemia.

Most hypoglycemic people go undiagnosed until later. But if your grandmother and your mother are both hypoglycemic—when you come crawling home in the middle of the second feature and think you are dying—they know exactly what is going on. They threw me down on the couch, made me eat a couple of small chunks of cheese and some orange juice, and told me to take a nap. Twenty minutes later, I woke up, and my education began.

Later, when I was studying to become a clinical hypnotherapist, the education was filled out to cover all of what happened... and the result. So this is one of the serious parts of this small book. This time, the tongue is NOT in my cheek.

The borderline hypoglycemic child goes to the Saturday matinée. To get there on time, they skipped lunch—just once. They bought their ticket and then bought a drink, some candy, or caramel corn.

They went into the large dark room and, during the cartoons, ate and drank most or all the sugar. The sugar converted to glucose, and during the first movie, the child's blood sugar spiked—big time. The adrenaline of having fun with the other kids didn't help—it burns a lot of the sugar.

Now here is where I was different. I didn't go with other kids to the movies. Only later did I ever do anything with other kids. Remember, when I moved to town and didn't stick to myself, I got beat-up. So, I was alone. And—I can almost hear a bunch of other people nodding. So, here comes the important part.

The kid is now into the second movie. The blood sugar probably peaked shortly after the opening credits. Within minutes, without a new supply of sugar, the system goes into free fall. As high as the peak—so comes the valley. Most medicos can tell you if your blood sugar drops below eighty, you need some help. Much lower and, the kid in the dark room, with a movie that now no longer makes any sense, and a body feeling worse than the flu—believes they are dying.

Even if they had been to the theater dozens of times—now it is a dark, scary, strange place… where they are dying. To a nine-year-old—it is a very scary thing.

Phobias are defined as irrational fears. It is not a learned, rational fear like crossing busy streets; you know cars can kill you, so you use the crosswalk and look both ways.

Phobias are acquired in a split second. Case in point: A child is holding the family pet bunny. They love the bunny. Lightning strikes the house, and they are thrown across the room at the same moment they had stroked the soft furry bunny.

Do they become afraid of lightning? Maybe. But the likelier fear is leporiphobia—the fear of rabbits or bunnies. Not just giant Easter costumed people, but Bugs Bunny on the TV, a rabbit's foot luck charm, or even drawings by other kids. Sometimes the phobia exacerbates the fear of all furry animals—Doraphobia. Not a good thing to have if you live in Manhattan.

So where are we with the kid in the dark, strange place who thinks they are dying? Rarely do they become Nyctophobic—but night can bring on some anxiety. What they become sums up over sixty percent of all phobic reactions—Agoraphobia. Literally, it is Greek for *marketplace*. In a broad term, it means wide-open spaces. But what it means to most is fear of going out of one's house.

It's not so much about the wide-open spaces. It's about the lack of support for when they need to be saved from dying. There are many who, when they feel safe to do so, will admit they know where every hospital, fire station, police station, or medical clinic is between their home and work or home and where they shop. If they must go somewhere new—it requires extensive research.

The part about the marketplace also translates into crowds. Being caught in the middle of a crowd, where you can't get out —is the same as not being able to get to somewhere you can be saved. In a large crowd, you can see people who are relaxed and enjoy the whole crush—and then there are the people with the panic-stricken look in their eyes. Those are the ones who need to get to the door.

It is estimated at least two in five suffer from varying levels of agoraphobia. Those who understand what is wrong do a lot better than those who don't—and certainly better than the dying kid in the dark theater.

As adults, they may function seemingly fine. But—one of the hallmarks of a hypoglycemic/agoraphobic is they will always be sitting on the aisle, and usually as near the door as possible. In a theater, this means the last three to five rows. In an airplane, it means up near the front—in front of the wing and always on the aisle. I know some see row seventeen is the cut-off. Lower row—or they won't go.

If any of this is sounding remarkably familiar and you have never taken a six-hour glucose test—see your doctor. Most hypoglycemia can be controlled by a protein weighted diet. Your doctor can set you on a course, and you will feel a lot better once you get your balance.

Yeah—a lot to learn for the scared kid in the dark.

Luckily, with Mom's and Grandma's help, I enjoy going to movies a lot. Back three rows, on the aisle—next to the door.

So... like the Oscars, I had been paying attention to only the leading and supporting characters. But moving into the house, across the narrow alley from the high school science building, which also faced the front lawn—I happened to stumble onto one of the minor supporting cast and found out just how much they could be a protagonist in their own right. I met Mr. Greene —the night janitor... or at least one of them. In the scope of the classical hero's journey, Mr. Greene would be the kindly mentor —for those who like *Middle Earth*... Gandalf the Gray.

Walt was wiping down the chalkboard from the dusty erasure to a solid deep green. During the day, the teachers wrote and wiped, wrote and wiped, and by the end of the day—anything written was only a shade or two away from blending in. On Friday nights, Walt assessed the conditions of the teacher's erasers and swapped them out for ones he had vacuumed, washed, and dried until they looked like new.

I'm sure—no, I'm positive—this is only one of the services he performed, which went well beyond what his job called for, but no teacher ever noticed—their erasers just always seemed to work better on Mondays. I pointed this out to four of my former teachers at my 20-year reunion. All of them remembered the clean erasers but were surprised they had not noticed it at the time. One of them laughed and said he now understood the concept of elves making shoes in the night.

I don't know what we talked about night after night. Still, I just remember it was a haven to go spend an hour or so doing a menial task like sweeping, wiping, dusting, straightening—and having someone I felt safe in asking questions, sharing my troubles, or just listening to his stories. They were few, but I remember feeling I was possibly the only person he had ever shared them with.

The man spent decades working in the buildings each night. About nine o'clock, he went down to the janitor's room. There were a beat-up table and a few chrome-tube chairs. Most of the seats were taped.

Sitting on the small burner over the pilot light were two cans. The bottom was a can of beans, or hash, or pork & beans, or soup—sitting on top of the soup can was an old can with no label. The top had been opened long ago. What was left of his morning's coffee was in there. They sat there for the first four hours of his shift, and the pilot light slowly warmed them up.

I only had to go there a few times to know every night it was the same. Leftover coffee and a can of warm food, eaten alone on a time-beaten, faded-green Formica and nickel-chrome table and chairs. The room was always warm and almost steamy—the three giant furnaces shared the space. He once pointed over his shoulder with his spoon at the furnace, which had just fired up. "Same boilers were on the Mighty Mo." He was talking about the USS Missouri—it was the only allude to his former Navy service. There was a certain grace to it.

The pink "dirt" they spread in a shaken line across the halls or basketball courts—according to Walt—is ground up scrap from making rubbers, tiny balls of paraffin, and a bit of sawdust. The combination attracts the dirt and dust—and down the main hall, would quadruple in volume. High school kids are filthy.

One day I got to thinking about what he had said—as I pushed half of my dust mop through the next pass of pink dirt. The paraffin I understood kind of waxed the floors. The sawdust was there just as a sort of lubricant. It was the other.

"What kind of rubbers?"

He stopped and turned. I knew the look. He had heard the question… It just didn't make sense.

I pointed at the pink dirt line on the floor. "You said it was made from sawdust, paraffin, and the scrap from making rubbers. Which kind of rubbers?"

His face gently morphed into a patronizing but kindly look. "The American kind." He turned back around and resumed pushing.

To this day, I don't know if he meant rubber boots, erasers, or condoms. For him, it sufficed. They were American.

Later, I found out he had served in the Pacific during WWII. But—I never heard him utter one word of ill-will about anyone. It was the best lesson he ever taught me.

One night, Walt had asked if I sold all the worms I gathered off the lawn. I told him I did. He suggested I might save some out of the Friday night's harvest, and he would take me fishing.

Now fishing was kind of a sore subject in our household. Many years before, my father had wanted to go fishing. He had a three-piece fly-rod. He also had a wife, four kids, and a dog. Only my mother had stayed out of the stream. He never went fishing again.

Walt taught me how to fish. How to fish the Owens River, and how to fish the small culverts under many of the town's driveways, where the strange irrigation trenches ran through the city. They were no more than a foot wide. The water was rarely over six- or eight-inches deep—but I pulled many a limit of perfect pan-sized brown trout out of the system.

He taught me how to wrap a big fat nightcrawler onto the oversized treble hook if you were fishing for dinner, or how a single feed is good on a barbless single hook if you are going to let the fish go. Another lesson—not all fish need to get eaten. Long before catch and release was popular.

His eyes, hand, and a whisper in the morning heat would point out the fat catfish rolling in the shadow of the overhanging grassy riverbank. Him holding my arm as the river eddied… and then letting go as if he had just released the trigger. My line racing out with three split shots on instead of two—set three feet back instead of one—it dropped into the river just before the eddy fumed and swelled to swallow the small splash. A minute later, I would be hauling on the reel and rocking back on the rod.

I caught a lot of fish over the years since. But the best lesson he ever taught me was fast, painful, and forever remembered.

Mom waved goodbye as we rolled off in his old green truck. About halfway down the street—South High School Lane—he asked when we needed to be back.

Trying on my cool tough kid persona, I answered. "My ol' lady said lunchtime was fine."

We weren't going fast. But I remember hitting the metal dashboard when he stopped.

"Get out."

"But I thou—"

"Get out."

I had all weekend—and his week of vacation to think about it. Think about what had happened—what I had said—and how he had reacted.

I cautiously entered the room as he was wiping the front board. He never looked around. He probably knew who it was the moment I opened the back door to the building, a floor below. I hated loud noises—so I didn't let the large, heavy steel doors bang shut.

I slipped into the desk at the back.

The sound of the twenty-some keys on their ring—attached to his belt on a clip—almost made a soft kind of music as he worked. The front board was slowly transforming from whitish green-yellow to dark green.

"Who is the person who carried you for nine months, and then screamed in pain as she gave birth to you?"

"My mother."

I'm not sure if someone passing in the hall could have heard our low voices. Walt wasn't a loud man. Even when he stood at one end of the basketball court and me at the other end—our conversations rarely got louder than a regular conversation.

"Who raise you?"

"Mom."

"Who is her mother?"

"Grandma Ruth."

"How old is she?"

I was stumped. "I don't know… old, I guess."

"Is she old enough to be your ol' lady?"

He turned.

"No."

"Remember that. No woman ever is. Not even… no… especially your wife."

Of all the women I dated when I was a biker—not one did I ever think of, much less refer to, as my ol' lady. And—by gosh—*never* my wife.

THE GUY IN THE SUIT, up in the office that is opened by the soft, very-worn key with the small round head—may have a master's degree or even a Ph.D.—but he's not always the smartest guy in the building. Maybe it's the reason they only trust him with a few keys—instead of the big wad of all the keys.

A LITTLE SIDE NOTE: About the janitor in any building—not the migrant cleaners who come and go—but the person with the huge wad of keys on their hip—the ones who can "feel" for the right key and find it the first time—if you ever think they are the low man on the totem pole, you are right.

The totem pole is not read like you think. The animal or guy on the bottom is supporting everyone else. Yeah, those poles would look silly with the eagle trying to support the turtle, fox, moose, and bear.

If you don't believe me—Google it. Look up what happens about the second week into a janitor strike. Portland, Oregon, Public School District had tried to replace all the guys who knew how to keep the old buildings running. The people who knew every lock and key. The ones who knew how to do a lot more than empty the trash cans. The ones who knew how to coax an extra twenty-years out of an antiquated furnace. The ones who knew how to clean erasers that lasted for generations of teachers.

By the time they hired the axed real janitors back, the school district had replaced five furnace systems, and dozens of locks were replaced where they had been removed because the minimum wage cleaners had taken them out instead of going through fifty keys to find the right one. Broken handrails were just unscrewed and left on the floor for kids to trip over—or step on the screws. It took over a year for the real janitors to fix all the mess the cheaper replacements had caused.

This lesson goes a lot further than just janitors.

If a person is helping you, treat them with respect—or be ready for the service you receive. That goes for tipping wait staff, acknowledging and thanking nurses in the middle of the night, thanking and tipping taxicab drivers, and information people in all aspects of society. If you want to see a shocked smile, thank the person at Costco or a market handing out samples. Not just a mumbled thank you, but a sincere "Thank you for being here and handing out samples."

A friend of mine—known for being cheap—talked up the concierge for some great seats to a show in Vegas. He slipped the guy a ten—for two of the hottest tickets in town. The next night, the concierge got them "some of the last tickets in town" for another hot show—row forty—and right behind one of two of the giant support columns in the entire building. They could hear the music, they could hear the magician talking—but they couldn't see any of the amazing magic tricks I enjoyed from the sixth row just to the side. I had slipped the concierge a fifty—twenty minutes before showtime.

As you read my books, you will understand it is not the high offices who get my respect—it is the people who work hard and move the day-to-day life forward. Look at a picture of the New York Stock Exchange. Those guys on the floor, shouting out numbers, throwing trash on the floor, and strutting around like life itself depended on them... make close to a million bucks a year. The janitor who cleans up all the shit each night, and then scrubs the toilets, polishes the brass, and wipes down all the surfaces for the next day of business... barely makes more than minimum wage, rides the metro out to Queens, walks eleven blocks to the fourth-floor walkup where he has to bang on the pipes to get the heat in the winter.

Before I leave Walt to clean more boards, here's a little side note about my graduating from high school—which probably shocked more than a few people other than myself.

When we graduated in Bishop, the graduation is done on the front lawn. My graduating class was 164 students. And 148 walked down the aisle. I cannot think of a more beautiful setting than under those giant elm trees. Unfortunately, the Dutch elm disease wiped them all out.

Family, friends, relatives, drunks, and other bored residents or curious tourists of Bishop, would sit or stand, watching the two-hour festival.

Blah, blah, blah… speeches, and then they call your name, hand you an empty folder, shake your hand, and you walk off to your seat. You have all seen this happen a gazillion times.

Two highlights for my graduation was Candy McCoy and Walt. Candy was a sweet, quiet girl. She was very pretty—blond with blue eyes and a smile warm enough to melt a ski slope—but one I didn't see a lot of. I just liked her. She had walked down the aisle with me in eighth grade. We, or I, lucked out, and we walked down the aisle again our senior night. As we stood at the top of the steps of the administration building, she leaned toward me and took my hand. She gave it a small, shy squeeze and whispered, "Here we are again." I could only smile. It was the most relationship or friendship we had—but she recognized it too.

As for Walt—I hadn't seen him in a few years. I didn't even notice if he was in the audience—I assumed he was probably cleaning the rooms on the second floor by then—probably the typing classroom—every machine got feather dusted, and then a cloth draped over them. For Walt, the ritual of caring for the typewriters was almost a holy thing. Each cover was draped by using two hands. As he taught me the ritual, he explained: Some of the greatest pleasures in this world came from the keys typing great books. I think he would have loved the idea of my ending up as a writer.

They called my name. I walked to the center—although he was smiling as he handed me the empty folder, he shook my hand—and I think Dr. Tanksly was as shocked as I was. I had gotten out of there in four years, and with most of my skin.

I held up the stupid folder and grinned like an idiot. Hell, I didn't even know where my parents were sitting. I was just taking the folder on the lamb. As I walked down those fateful three steps, there standing at the bottom was Walt. Work boots, green-faded work pants, and a white T-shirt. He was only taking a break. His hand was out. His eyes were a little misty. He never had to say a word. I nodded my thanks—the moment meant a lot to both of us.

Friends for me in those days were few and far between. Some came and went—a few had a life-long impact.

Stewart Edel was one of those who had a profound impact. Not only physically as well as mentally and socially—but he also had an influence that eventually led to my becoming a writer.

Seventh grade is an interesting time. Some of the boys and most of the girls have just about reached their eventual height. Stewart was the tallest in the class, and I was a close second or third. Stewart was already over six-foot, and I was closing on an inch or so shorter. The combination of the two could have proven fatal.

Recess is when hormones and adrenaline combine to put physical play into hyper-drive. The winter day on the playground was no exception. The ground was frozen, the monkey bars were hard, and the chin-up bar was just at the right, or wrong, height.

I was sitting on Stewart's shoulders as we were being the big monster chasing the others around the monkey bar area. And then I wasn't.

Lead blue-gray sky one moment—bright hospital lights the next. And then the dark room as they took lots of x-rays. Hard head, solid neck, and strong back—but the prognosis was, in the words of Dr. Bob Denton, "Really mucked it up good this time."

During the week of green gelatin and mystery food as bland as the unsalted mashed potatoes, Stewart and his father came to visit. He felt horrible. Other than the persistent headache from the concussion and the tweaked strained muscles in the back and neck, they kept shoving drugs into me for—I felt, well, just glowing. The visit was a cherry on top of the mashed potatoes.

Just having Stu stop by was enough, but he had felt the need to bring a peace offering. He knew I liked the writings of Mark Twain—and he had his dad buy the book *Roughing It*. The huge volume is still here in my office. *To my friend—sorry about the fall—I hope we are still friends—Stewart.*

We still are, Stu.

STEWART'S FATHER was the foremost authority on the California Desert Tortoise. Not because he was a biologist, but because he was a state highway engineer who brought home an injured tortoise one day and nursed it back to health. As highways were built and roads expanded, the workers stopped throwing injured tortoises back out into the desert to die. Soon the Edel front gate acquired the accurate sign "*Danger—wild reptiles at large.*"

One of the side effects of Mr. Edel's concern for the reptiles was his power of observation and interest in keeping a journal. Soon, his concern made its way to the in-house organ (magazine) of the State Division of Highways. They asked him to write a short article about the tortoise. What they got was a lot of commentary about how important the reptile was to the fragile ecosystem of the desert—and how many were slaughtered each year during construction and maintenance.

His article got the attention of the powers that be, and soon it became routine to clear a construction site of all tortoises and relocate them at least a mile away in the desert—but dispersed with a minimum of a hundred yards between each tortoise, so they weren't competing for food. Yes, he had a wad of keys on his hip.

By the end of the seventh grade, the Edels and my family had moved out to the developing West Bishop. They had a large lot backing up to a large irrigation ditch. (Large is defined by the ditch being about eighteen inches wide and about a foot deep and flowed almost all year.) They dug a pond in the spacious back yard—for fish—the tortoises could have cared less about water, but there was lots of grass to graze on.

Stewart's dad had become an expert about how deep he had to pour concrete walls so that the tortoises didn't burrow their way out. (If I remember right, he poured a four- or six-foot bed, and then a four-foot standing wall projecting one foot above the ground.) The back border was the irrigation ditch—they never went in the water. As he discovered things, he wrote more articles in different journals, which were published by university presses, reptile societies, and the like.

After years of having the little guys crawling about and occasionally entertaining us boys, he found out every time he went to research something about tortoises that he already knew more than what he found. Eventually, he was at the University of California at Davis and was doing some serious research about the respiratory system of the hibernating tortoise. He was at a stall in his research, so he asked for some help. He needed to consult with someone knowledgeable—an expert. He sent out inquiries.

He got several replies. All of them pointed to the acknowledged foremost authority on the California Desert Tortoise—and as luck would have it—he lived in Bishop. Jack laughed and lined his fireplace with the letters suggesting he get in touch with himself.

He and his tortoises were on their own.

Stewart's best friend forever was Fred Dock. Fred would be best summed up as stocky with thick black Clark Kent glasses. Beyond the body type, he was Clark Kent and a faithful friend. I was graced to be part of their friendship—a small part, but a part.

I had no idea how big the part really was until our twenty-year reunion. I was out on disability from being hit by a truck.

I DRINK COFFEE AND MAKE SHIT UP

Between numerous surgeries, more than a ton of ice, and more sleep than I want to think about—I had offered to track down and call people from our class. You would think none of the other classmates had ever seen a phone bill for over three hundred dollars before.

Most reunions of Bishop High are doing good when they get a fifty percent turn-out. Our twentieth reunion, we hit in the eighties. We were all shocked. I was simply happy to be recovered enough to make it.

At the Sunday pancake breakfast in the park, several people came to thank me for calling and cajoling them into coming. Then Stewart and Fred came down near the stream where I was. I was having a hard time just taking it all in. I had been one of the least popular in school. I was the loner who got out of class, got on his motorcycle, and left. Some or a lot of people thought I was stuck-up or something—it was just the shyness had taken hold. I had nothing to say. Or was afraid to say it.

The boys were kind of shy and kept looking at each other as I thanked them for coming. Stu had driven down from Northern California, but Fred had traveled all the way from the Chicago area. I hadn't realized they hadn't seen each other since their weddings.

Finally, I asked these men acting like the seventh graders we had once been, what was going on.

Fred kicked at the dirt and looked at the muddy streambed for an answer. Part of the answer was the red creeping up out of his collar and headed for his ears. I'll bet even today that his habit has never changed. Or, I'd like to think he still endures—it may sound strange to say it's charming—but there is no other term for it.

Stewart cleared his throat—he always was the mouthpiece for the two. "We only came—because you called and asked us to."

I noticed his foot was kicking at the dirt also. Three grown men—so many years later—still kicking at the dirt... old friends are older, but still the same boys.

IN THE LAST days of the nineteenth century, the city of Los Angeles was drying up. A man by the name of Mulholland looked at the Owens Valley. With its majestic mountains and fertile valley of alfalfa, apples, oranges, pears, apricots, grapes, nuts, and other trainable foods, the Owens Valley was rightly called the Little Switzerland of America. The closest to Switzerland now is the architecture of the Dutch bakery. The majestic orchards, when I was growing up there, were nothing more than six-inch tall rotting stumps in long rows. Mulholland and L.A. had long ago killed the valley by taking all the water.

Owens Lake—once a quarter the size of Lake Tahoe—is now an alkaline hardpan. Mono Lake was soon to be the same until a law was passed, establishing a minimum water level guaranteeing the water isolation and, therefore, survival of Negit Island. It is one of only two nesting sites for the western seagull. The other is the Great Salt Lake in Utah.

I only throw this in because the desert I grew up in—was manmade. So along with the sage and bitterbrush, there were the strange huge fields of small stumps. There were canals, dry of any water for half a century. Where once there was a thriving cattle community, only a few thousand head now exist in the outer areas—most owned by families who never sold out to L.A. for a few pennies per acre for their water rights or land. Those ranches are why a pro rodeo still exists in Bishop. There is also Mule Days—which I'll get to later.

Running down the middle of the valley is the Owens River. There are a few bridges that cross the river. East Line Street is one of the important ones. If your mom drove a truck or VW van, she would pile a bunch of you kids and the inner tubes which were over-inflated to fat, into the van, and drop you off at Line Street. Then she could drive to Safeway or Joseph's Market, shop, take the groceries home, have lunch, and then drive to Collin's Hole and wait for you in the cool shade of the big cottonwood trees.

Collin's Hole was a cool place—and not just because of the trees. At the end of about five or six miles, which meandered for probably ten or more miles, the river took a tumble down about twenty feet of rapids, which were about half a block long or shorter. A fun bumpy ride at the end of two or three lazy hours in the sun—floating the river—usually, we had to drag the tubes back up a few times for the fun ride.

FOR MORE ON the river and the Owens Valley, I made it one of the quiet but powerful characters in my Thorny Wallace series, starting with *Death in the Valley*.

ARROWHEADS WERE all over the desert floor—if you knew where to look. Dick Swanson was one of those people. He looked like a broken-over old man wizened by life and the sun. In a way, he was. His goatee and gaunt face gave him the likeness of a kindly old goat. But he also had a mean look which served him well.

Few knew he was chronologically a decade younger than he appeared. Those friends close enough knew he had once been about a foot taller, and a bodybuilder. An auto accident had broken his back in seven places. He had a ring on his finger with the number seven on it. Most thought it was for the "lucky seven"—the reality was it reminded him he wasn't the bull he was when he was twenty-seven.

The Swans (rhymes with once) worked at Tony's Union 76 station from about six pm to six am. I don't remember if he had a day off or not. He had almost nothing to spend his paycheck on, which gave him a pocket of cash. When a flatlander from L.A. would beg for a tank of gas to get home, it didn't matter to the Swans if they were a ski bum, a hunter, or fisherman. They usually had something to trade for the five-dollar tank of gas. Gas was about thirty-five cents a gallon at the Union—about a dime more than any other station in town—which were all closed for the night.

For less than five bucks, the Swans took pistols (usually loaded), rifles, shotguns, and jewelry. Most of it he turned around and unloaded by the next weekend, so he could look the returning tourist in the eye and honestly tell them he sold their whatever for only a few bucks more than the tank of gas had cost him. If you were looking for a hunting rifle or shotgun—Dick was the man to know.

When he broke his back, he was all stoved up. A wise doctor with a bad hair-lip suggested he walk and maybe bend over occasionally. The exercise led him to hunting for arrowheads. The man's collection was legendary. And the ones he showed off weren't even his best pieces. He sent a few large trays down to the history museum in L.A. They said it was the most amazing and complete collection of Piute arrowheads they had ever seen. Every single point was almost a perfect specimen.

The Swans just laughed. He had sent them his rejects. His best stuff was hidden under his bed in his trailer. Hidden in the floor were amazing collections of guns and jewelry.

When he didn't show up for work one night, nobody thought anything about it. But a few days later, the sheriff had to drill out the lock on his trailer door to get in. He had passed in his sleep. Funny how by the time the city police showed up, there was no trace of any arrowheads, guns, or jewelry—just a beat-up old gold ring on his finger with a seven on it.

I'm not pointing fingers—there are plenty of people in the town to do it for me. I just miss stopping by in the middle of the night and talking to the old goat. I revived him and his mentoring heart for *Death in the Valley*. The being was too great just to let slip away. His plain-speaking became Thorny's grandfather, but the mentor became Ulysses.

One night, in the late 1960s, he had made an exception. The tourist wasn't a hunter or fisherman—they were an artist who had been up painting some of the Sierra Mountains. Dick asked, "What were the most important paints in the man's case." The man had told him they were all important. A few days later, my mother got a bag full of some of the best oil paint.

It wasn't who knew the Swans—it was who he cared about... and why.

Years later, she found out he liked goat cheese—something she made. He was set—until he died.

As I said before, Mom had a printing press. Everyone who knew us—knew about the press. If you attended a Boy Scout leadership meeting at Bill Charlton's house—there were probably numerous large trays of freshly printed business cards, or note cards, or Christmas cards lying about to dry. Most evenings, there were two or three runs of stuff laid out. Don't touch.

One of the other things about our household was non-stop jokes. A pun a day keeps the dead brain cells away. Almost no joke was off-limits. Even off-color was fine—if it wasn't off-color just for off-color sake. We kids loved when our father went off to some seminar or meeting. He would come back a few days later with at least three or four juicy, racy jokes. If Mom could discuss internal organs and interesting stuff that she typed up at the hospital—Dad could tell raunchy jokes.

One night, there was some kind of Boy Scout meeting going on. Mom and I had prepped for the best joke ever. The men were spread out around the living room. Soon after the meeting started, I delivered the second tray of cards we had printed the night before. Some of the men who were close leaned over to see what Mom and I were working on. The attention was mild, and not more than just a reflex. Business cards are boring.

After we had been printing for a while, the trays of Christmas cards came out. Along about the end of the first hour, Mom laid out some trays of cards we had been given. They were incredibly detailed, and the green ink was close to the last set of trays.

Timing is everything.

My father had figured they would break for some coffee and fresh-baked cookies around eight-ish. At about ten minutes before eight, Mom took out a tray of fresh five-dollar bills she had bought for just this night.

She took up the tray of the first business cards and put down the fives. It was so routine that nobody even seemed to notice Mom had even been in the room—business meeting as usual.

Then someone noticed the Christmas cards didn't look like Christmas cards anymore. They glanced back at the meeting as my father asked them a question. When processing the asked question, it slows down the back of the mind that is having a hard time coming up with an answer to the picture which just wasn't fitting.

She has a printing press… She does do some exceptionally fine work… She just printed those cards over there using the green ink…

Soon more than a couple of the men had noticed. Even after the nervous laughter had turned to comradely laughter—a few of the men still had to go touch the ink. Just to make sure.

Dry, but did she…?

Things aren't always as they appear. Great way to twist a plot—and it applies to characters as well. Or, on occasion—a real human or two.

WANTING to believe is a powerful force. So, everyone was a twitter, which means a rumor had started at one end of town, and before you could drive down Main Street, the rumor was already at the other end—or so it would seem. Actually, it took almost two days to spread through town. The frontman (nobody knew what the title really meant) for Sam the Sham and The Pharaohs, of *Wolly Bully* fame, was in town. He was holed up on secret business at the Best Western. He was running up a tab at any restaurant that would let him. Rumors were running rampant they would be putting on a concert at the Fair Grounds—name a date.

After a week, the maid went into the room to find the only word of truth was: Sham. The guy had flown the coop, having dined on almost nothing but steaks and lobster, steak sandwiches, and steak and eggs. The people who got the real stake were the restaurants and the Best Western.

The funny part about it came the next spring. The real road manager, along with Domingo "Sam" Samudio, came to Bishop in a bid to throw a concert during the Tri-County Fair. The police chief and the mayor grabbed the guys by the metaphorical pants and neck and threw them out of town.

Bishop wasn't going to get caught a second time.

Meanwhile, the Union Carbide tungsten mine, just north of town, had a new engineer. The man was a delightful person by the name of Max Schnelling. The town swells had fallen in love with Max. No reason not to—he was charming, intelligent, good with us kids—and a master bridge player.

He took my smart oldest brother to a match or meet or whatever they call them—and the sixteen-year-old kid—walked away with masterpoints to his name by the end of the night. Was my brother brilliant? No—he just followed directions.

This kind of stuck in some craws, but he was so debonair.

And smooth, and slick, and very smart—but one of the things he was not—was taking advantage of anyone. In fact, he was there just to enjoy himself, and if it meant others around him had a good time as well... so be it.

Over the beautiful summer, he became a fixture around the pool at the Dentons. He didn't swim, but he wasn't beyond throwing a kid in the pool for fun. He also would clench his hands together so you could put your foot in there, and then he would throw you in a backflip into the pool.

That was... until one kid came down and hit their head on the side.

I woke up with a sizeable hair-lipped smile in my face. "So... you hit your head and went bonk." Bob was never one to be dramatic about an injury when he could just be funny instead. I smiled and just walked funny for a few days.

It doesn't bother me anymore very much, much, much...

To MAKE up for such a fiasco start of the summer, Max suggested he take Betty Denton, and us seven kids, to Disneyland, and maybe Knott's Berry Farm too. Betty would bunk in with the three girls, and Max with the four boys. Actually, Max got a connecting room so he could get some sleep.

So off we went. Only as an adult did I realize what a huge financial offering it was to take us on a week tour of the two big parks of Southern California. Betty said later she offered to help, but Max had thanked her and told her it was all on him. The man really did have a great heart.

Two adults and seven kids—it would make a great comedy movie, except nothing really happened to stand out. We all had a great time. We spent a couple of days at Disneyland, and then a day at Knott's Berry Farm. Then Max decided we needed some education, so it was off to Marine land (now a large set of buildings by the sea or long gone).

We went to Chinatown. We went to Hollywood. We went to

the La Brea tar pits—until we all got the creepy idea and remembered how much Max loved to throw us kids in the pool—so we backed away and went back to the cars.

So, you're scratching your head and wondering what this has to do with this book or my writings...

It does, and it doesn't. Remember when I said "THE" family vacation was in the summer of 1959? So here it was a few years later, and us four kids got a taste of what families mean when they say a vacation. We were a couple of miles from my one uncle, seventy from the thirteen families in Riverside, and a hundred from my uncle in Santa Barbara—we visited nobody. The two adults were on the kid's time schedule. It was simply weird.

Do I resent our own family vacation, ala my father? No—we didn't know any different—until the summer with Max.

What those two vacations became in my mind is the definitive case of what you know, and then being exposed to what others know—neither is right or wrong. Both are right, and both are just what they are... different.

In writing scenes like the pivotal conversation with Hooker and his sister in *Night Vision*, it ends up being about how two people chose two paths and grew to different ends. I was just graced to see those two paths, so I could write with understanding the angst and resolve that comes with the understanding of both just being paths of choice—no right, no wrong.

Do I carry a bit of a grudge about 1959, because it wasn't the same as 1964? Maybe, but I think it is more complicated—but it is still a good tool in the desk.

SO FINALLY, Max upped and vacated. Well, just disappeared in the middle of the night. He quit the job he had no training for—but was exceptional at. He had streamlined a lot of what had not been working for a long time—even though he had no college degree, much less an engineering degree.

His name was really Max, just not Schnelling. The German term "*Mach schnell*" means "Do it fast"—or pull a fast one. Max did—but he did it nice and slow and with a lot of fun and pleasure.

Many years later, I looked him up. He was happily married to a minor star from the black and white era. They were both incredibly happy in the Hollywood Hills. While I was visiting, a little dog wandered into the back yard. Max called his neighbor to tell him about his dog. A couple of minutes later, there was a knock on the door. Max handed me the poodle and told me he thought I might enjoy giving the dog back.

I opened the door to find Vincent Price standing there in bathrobe and slippers. He apologized for the disturbance. Silly me, I just smiled and said the pleasure was all mine. Max asked me why I didn't invite Vincent in and ask him for his autograph. He had remembered our conversation in the car on the long drive home in the middle of the night. He had asked me if I could meet only one movie star—who would I want it to be? Lon Chaney, Bella, and Boris were already gone—which left only Vincent.

I smiled at Max and told him—I had already gone to Disneyland with the better actor.

2

GETTING STARTED OR CHAPTER 4,783.2B OR YOU MIGHT CALL IT THE FOREWARD OR THE IMPORTANT CHAPTER YOU NEVER READ

Halfway through my life, I realized I was at the peak. My new career, and everything from that moment on, was downhill—and would stink for a while. Wait. Stink is too mild a word… It would reek with an eye-searing burn only gorilla piss in the steaming mountain jungle of Rwanda can produce.

You may wonder what sitting at ten thousand feet on the side of a volcano has to do with writing, but for me, it was everything. I'm not suggesting for every would-be writer to go out and get a young mountain gorilla to piss all over his or her back, but it is life—and perspective-altering.

The entire way up the Virunga volcano, our guide strongly stressed that we would be close to the gorillas—do *not* try to touch them. I'm sure my mind was asking the usual smartass question. "Close, like across a football field close, or close as in the young woman at the other end of the subway car, who will mace you if you get closer?"

It didn't matter. I was there to take great photos. Getting killed by a five-hundred-pound silverback was not on my bucket list.

The guide was six feet from me when the eighty pounds of

young female gorilla came across the steep mountainside. Straight at me. The guide's eye grew larger and larger. We were silent—we both knew I was about to be torn apart. I knew the strength from playing with an Orangutan. This gorilla already had the muscle strength to rip my well-developed arms from my body. And, if she had any trouble… the five-hundred-pound silverback sat not thirty-feet away. I whispered to the other photographers. "Get this on film. I'm about to die."

The "silver" on a silverback (leader of the group) is not an age-induced trait. It comes from the females of the collective urinating on the back of a young male who they want to be the next leader. In a way, they are choosing their next mate—kind of like asking the male to the ultimate Sadie Hawkins dance. The silverback might be the "big guy," but the society is a collective matriarch—the women run it.

So, when this little slip of a girl reached out, it was with a featherlight touch. She wanted me to bend forward so she could access my back. Silly ol' Baer. I thought she just wanted to get past. Then she started rubbing her butt all over my back… which became hot and wet. The silverback snorted, and I'm convinced to this day, he was laughing. I know she was.

After, she wandered off to smoke a cigarette or munch on some grass or take a nap. With a doltish look on my face, I sat trying to make order of what had just happened, and of my life.

PHOTOJOURNALISM IS AN INTERESTING PROFESSION. First, you need to create an image that tells a story. Next, you need to understand the image's story enough to retell in words the image is telling. Your words need to help tell the image's story—better. A good storyteller spins the tale well enough until the image is the support for the words. In a way, the title should be a writer-photoist. Either way, you are a reporter of an event—even if it happened to you.

Everyone has the potential to be a reporter. Yes, everyone. We grab a fork wrong, and it flips in the air and lands sticking upright in another person's plate of spaghetti. We laugh, and maybe tell a few other people... for years. It's funny and makes a funny story. Perhaps it's the first date, and you're still telling the story of how you impressed your spouse of fifty years, at your anniversary party. Or, maybe you use it as a line in a book where the spy uses the distraction to draw their gun with their offhand and shoots the other spy. After all, Han *did* shoot first.

We experience events, incidents, or just a tumble. For most, these are just experiencing and soon forgotten. But, for a writer, these are material for stories. The color of real life is what imbues fiction with body and soul. It makes words become storytelling.

The same holds true for characters. When a character is little more than a name and description, they are only good for being killed off in the first or third chapter. However, build the character around your sixth-grade teacher. The feckless Ichabod Crane, with the shaving cut where he couldn't grow a five o'clock shadow to rival his student's. He can mumble his way past his pedophilic lechery, on his way to becoming a worthwhile villain. Or at least until you kill him in chapter forty-seven.

This little book isn't so much a pedagogical how-to-write, as much as it is a tumbling romp through memories that are tools and guidelines for my writing. Much of these are of childhood—the foundation of future actions, intents, and responses. I don't write vampire shit because I have no clue what another person's blood would taste like. (But I do have plenty of experience tasting my own.) I also never bit anyone—that I know of. But, if I did write a vampire story, I would have to write it from the perspective of the one getting bitten. I owe the knowledge to my dear sister, who practiced the act on my young beautiful body and skin several times. She never did fight fair.

Someone once asked me what genre I wrote in. We were sitting in an expensive restaurant located in uptown Seattle. Shye Ryder, who I co-wrote a book with, interjected. She pointed out to the street, saying he has his own genre. *I do?*

Shye grabbed my hand and squeezed for me to shut up while she continued. "See the pretty, freshly painted, white lines?" The woman nodded. "He doesn't write about those."

Tossing her mane of chestnut hair, she waved her open hand along the wall of windows. "See the lovely warm street, filled with gleaming stylish cars, beautiful people rushing to and from work, or just shopping for newer and shinier trinkets?" The woman nodded again. "He doesn't even see those—except at a distance." *I nodded… it was true.*

Shye's index finger became almost laser as she pointed at the opposite corner. "But do you see the corner curb? The one where the woman is wearing the Jones of New York three-piece suit and Jimmy Choo's? Below it, there is grit and gravel mixed with off castings of the uncaring pretty people. *That* is his genre. The people who are the thrown-away trash, the grit in the day-to-day. The larger people, who are the gravel on the smooth corners of life, who make you lose your footing and twist your ankle because you weren't paying attention. The homeless loose sand your tires spin-out and crash from—because you were going too fast. But it is those: gravel, grit, dirt, trash—those are his people, his genre, the stories he tells. Not the pretty—but the ugly or commonplace. Scars aren't surface decolorizations—they have depth in their stories. The smooth airbrushed faces in supermarket magazines change every week. What was relevant or pretty this week is passé next week and forgotten by next year. But the people who are the grit… unforgettable—for a lifetime. His genre. The grit people—where they struggle to live, what they do to survive, and the heart beating inside."

Well, here's to grit. I know it well.

3

PUTTING IT ALL TOGETHER

Once you have a few boxes of old experiences, you can take a few out, throw them together in a blender and stir up some shit. Trust me. This isn't like baking a cake or cooking a turkey. This is a lot more like making a "berry" cobbler the Baer way.

In my front yard, we have four blueberry bushes, which are about forty years old. I'm old school... throw a bunch of shit on them. Then we were out at a blueberry farm... and they were spreading sawdust everywhere. I asked and was told: "Douglas Fir... you can't give them enough acid."

I have a small woodshop and work with much Doug Fir. Every huge bag from the dust collector goes on my blueberries with a bunch of shit. If I had access to dried sheep shit, I would layer it about six-inches thick.

In short—we get forty to sixty pounds of blueberries every year. So here is my recipe.

9" x 13" Pyrex pan—well buttered.
   Pour in about 9-pounds of blueberries until the pan is heaped.

Put in the cold oven, turn to 425° for about 15-minutes.

Get out the white sugar, butter, and go look in the liquor cabinet. Hmmm, dark rum, light rum, Kirshwasser (a clear brandy made from cherries… makes the flavor of all fruit sing).

I was feeling summery, so Kirsch, light rum, and a splash of Nellie and Joe's Key Lime juice. A splash of each into a water glass… so it's only about 2-ozs of liquor.

When the dinger goes off… pull out the warm berries and fold in a ½ stick or so of real butter with a ¼ cup or so of white or brown sugar. (Yup… you noticed… I was cooking on the fly.)

Keep folding as you drizzle the booze over the mix… NO TESTING.

Stick in oven and set timer for 30-minutes.

Whip up some runny Bisquick batter… use 7up instead of water. You'll need about ½ to a full cup of batter… At the 30-minute dinger, drizzle the top leaving some holes. If you're me, the batter is in the shape of a W for University of Washington. (After I gold leaf the W with 23.75kt edible gold—it makes my wife happy.)

Set timer for 12-minutes and keep checking until golden-brown and the berries are bubbling.

I've used rhubarb with berries (but you need to add a lot more sugar). A mix of black, blue, rasp, and huckleberries. No alcohol, more alcohol, sugar, honey, agave, no batter, whole batter, and everything between. You can't screw up a cobbler. But when it's perfect… it is heaven.

So, here is what doing the same in short form (short story/writing) is like.

In short form, your dish needs all the succulence of a longer story, but you have fewer words. If you write sparsely, you end with a broth that tastes like tainted water. So, you need to accost the senses with everything: sight, sounds, smells, tastes, perception, prejudices, understandings, social twists, morals, breaking morals, and misbehaving because it just feels wrong.

- So, we start with a socially charged time—1966 and civil rights.
- Get comfortable with day-to-day living in an all-white small town.
- Charge the air—hot, sticky, stinky, summer.
- Twist the perception—told through the eyes of a young boy.
- Throw in some "yuck" factor—a large scab ripe for picking at… in a small crowded café.
- Now, turn up the temperature on the simmering kettle…

Enjoy. I wrote this the summer of 2005, during the 40th anniversary of the Watts riots.

4

COZY CONFRONTATION

It was the summer I had the best "picking" scab I've ever had when the tourist stumbled into the Cozy Grill. I'd scraped the Hades out of my left arm up on Hellerman Cliffs. Bobby Teals and Blinkey Blinkman had been with me, sliding down the sun-scorched sandhills on sheets of brown pasteboard, until I hit the big rock and gravel patch. The sumbitch had bled all the way to Doc Weller's office on Elm Street.

I'd thought it hurt bad. And then, Nurse Richards started scrubbing the wound with a brush and yellow soap. I didn't know which I wanted more—to know how to swear real good and be able to or just pass out.

It made me feel better when Doc Weller put a big white dressing on it nobody could miss. It looked great, like a war wound or something. It was just too bad school was out for the summer.

I half paid attention as he told me what I should and shouldn't do to take care of it. But then, as we started to walk out of the backroom, he put his big warm hand on my shoulder and gave me the best news.

"Well, Mickey," he confided, "I think you got yourself a real 'picker' there." Ol' Doc Weller was a man's kind of doctor. He really understood what was important to us "men." Well... boys. I smiled up at him and strutted out of the office, into the sunshine of attention in all my macho glory, the wounded warrior. It was great.

Doc Weller had been light in his prognosis. It wasn't a good picker. It was the best picker ever. And "picking" was exactly what I was doing when the tourist stumbled in from the hard baking summer sunshine.

He just stood there, as the wire spring slapped the door up against his heels and butt. Silence choked the air of the lunchroom as twenty pairs of eyes opened wide, and several mouths dropped open and froze. The 'gater choking hum of the two wobbling greasy ceiling fans was the only noise or noticeable movement in the place. The stranger's eyes slowly grew accustomed to the dim lighting struggling its way through the windows, long painted over with dirty grease.

Blinkey nudged me under the table. I nudged him back. "What's wrong with his skin?" he whispered. I stared. Harry Woo, the cook at the D & B Brookside Dinner House, had a kind of yellowish skin. Rudy Mandrello, the ramrod out at the Diamond Bar XT, was half Apache and had a pock-ruptured red-purple face. But a black face? I'd never seen one.

"I don't know. Maybe it's oil or dirt," I whispered back, ignoring the crisp starched white shirt softly crinkling as he moved toward the counter. Pa gave me a look. I knew the look.

"Excuse me. Is someone sitting here?" The butter-soft voice pointed out a vacant seat next to Dex Dexler. The sound rattled through the café like a galvanized cannon shot.

The large dirt farmer in bib overalls growled. "My brother is —when he gets here." I couldn't believe my ears. Dex's only brother, Tyler, was cold in the ground three years if it was a day, and everyone knew it. Further, I'd never known Dex to lie.

Pointing to the seat covered with newspapers, on the other

side of Dex, and the only other empty seat at the small, time-worn painted counter, the black man asked, "Is this seat taken?"

"That's mine." Dex grunted.

The man opened his mouth to speak as his left palm rose slightly, then resolved, dropped his hand, closed his mouth, and looked around. All other eyes quickly became interested in the food being shoved into quiet mouths.

All other eyes except Blinkey's, mine, and "Cap" Yankalinsky, owner, cook, waiter, dishwasher, sweep out, and the town's Polish Jew. The man leaned against the "Tally" post, with a spatula in his right hand folded into his left arm. Quiet. Passive. Waiting. His dark iron eyes reflecting nothing and soaking up everything.

All tables were taken by the late lunch crowd lingering to escape the midday bake-off. From our vantage point of the biggest table, set off in the corner from the rest, Blinkey and I could watch the strange stirrings and behaviors of the men. Each came under the study of the stranger's dark eyes.

Politics and racial tensions were beyond the understanding of a ten-year-old boy in the summer of '66. The names Selma and Montgomery meant nothing to me in my all-white town. They were just names. Words. Meaningless words. Words occasionally uttered right before a disgusted spit of chew.

The stranger's eyes searched, looking for a way out. Like a hunter who is holding the mouth of the crocodile closed and dare not let go. He had entered boldly, a door stepped through, expecting refreshment and escape from the summer hell, and found only purgatory.

My father's back and shoulders rolled as he looked long and hard at Blinky and me. His right shoulder rolled, itching the large old scar on his back against the stiff patch sewn onto his shirt which read, Honey Man, Septic Installation & Pumping. He'd gotten the scar two winters before while cleaning the city jail's "Honey Pot." The infection almost killed him.

His fork and knife floated in his hoary, work-enlarged hands.

Mom called it "continental" eating, with your fork up-side-down in your offhand. But pa ate that way 'cause his right hand was little better than a vise to open and close since he came home from the war.

Pa rested his fork on the edge of his plate, gentle like, quietly studying us boys, mulling, and then softly half-turned in his seat.

The stranger's eyes snapped to the movement like a cornered cat under a bed. He took in every detail of my father—the scattered bald patches on the right side of his head. The purple and gray scars crawl up from his neck along his face—the mush where his right eye and ear used to be, and into his prematurely white hair. He saw the claw, still clamping the dinner knife. He noticed the special boot, the Honey Man shirt, and the possible smell it ordained.

This man knew my father. He knew him well. Yet they were strangers. Their eyes met. The two or three seconds were like hours. The silence was choking. My father pointed at the empty chair with his knife. One second, two. The man moved forward.

Pa turned around, and taking up his fork, gave us one of those looks. We sat stunned. No one ever sat with my father.

The black man pulled out the chipped, brown painted chair as his buttery soft voice almost whispered, "Thank you, sir." His white starched shirt rustled damply, and his tan chinos sighed across the chair as he sat. Then, as if seeing us boys for the first time, he smiled.

> He had a great white smile, like sheets on a clothesline shining in the summer sun. The heat of the smile washed over me. The heat you get from sitting in front of the kitchen belly stove in December, eating Tollhouse and oatmeal cookies after you've brought in the wood without being told. The warm feeling coming from a cat lying on your chest in front of the fire, while your folks talk and giggle softly in the kitchen. Friendly. Secure. Giving, never asking. A smile to remember, always.

5

A HIGHER EDUCATION

High school isn't always about the classes. Sometimes the education comes from odd places.

Let me clear the air before we delve into the deep end of raging hormones and other antisocial behaviors.

By my freshman year, if I'm not on the back of my brother's motorcycle, I'm riding the bus, thumbing a ride, or walking the two miles to school. No excuses, but I was a solid student—a solid D student… and occasionally, a fanciful D- student.

Was I dumb? No. Smart? If testing in the genius range and turning in consistent 1.0 work can be construed as smart—then yeah. By the tests, I should be handing in 4.0 grades and wowing the masses. But I loved the test—because who studies for an IQ test. And I hated homework. And having to sit in a room with people.

No. I heard you say everyone hates homework. But it's not true. People "hate *doing* homework." Which infers they are doing the homework—I hated homework. So I just didn't do it. No matter what I got on tests, I was never doing better than a C. So why try? I was bored out of my mind. There were few exceptions to this rule of no homework. I'll tell you about Dick Arnold in a minute.

I remember a few things about my freshman year —damn few.

It was the year the new drama teacher in town popped out the tidbit of "on his death, Shakespeare had willed his best bed to his friend Bacon. His wife got the second-best bed—the one with the knothole in the headboard."

So, in one short statement, I learned good old Will and Bacon were lovers and gay. It gave a whole different spin on *Mid-Summer's Night's Dream*. It also secured my interest for the next four years in drama.

It was two years later I learned if you're the young stud drama teacher in a tiny town, a few of the students and even more of the mothers were yours to bed—while your wife was off in Vegas screwing her boss. Titillating at the time, but fodder for future plot intrigue later.

It was my first introduction to complicated relationships. They didn't look right, weren't right, and sometimes were more than presented. If you have been following my crime series, The Southside Hooker series, you now know where the character Uncle Willie comes from.

If playwrights had been respected, Shakespeare would have been knighted. But, in his day, he was little more than a porn monger and one step above a pocket-pincher of a guttersnipe. Exactly where most of society in the midseventies held homosexuals. As I've noticed, the stranger and more twisted a sexual relationship seems on paper, the more commonplace they are in real life, or accepted by readers.

While on the subject, Bishop, the town I grew up in, had and has a population of about three-thousand people. Statistically, it means there would be about three hundred lesbians, gay, bisexual, transsexuals, queers, or just inquisitive (LGBTQI) roaming around in the intense little valley. (If they add more to the LGBTQI tent—it's going to break my little keyboard.)

In a small town, most people know most other people. You may think you are getting away with a fling or an affair, but trust me, many people know. (More on that later) They don't care what, when, or who you are doing—they just want to know about it.

Our family was mentally open. Mom was artistic, and my sister and I had the bent also. From an early age, I remember most of the artists and want-to-be artists floating in and out of our home and lives. In this creative culture, we had most of the guys and their boyfriends place their shoes under Mom's table in the backyard for dinner. I never gave a second thought to this guy and that guy being in a liaison—I was never taught it was wrong. Like the song in South Pacific—you must be taught to hate.

My first crush was on my fifth-grade teacher. She lived with her "friend," who was the high school girl's gym teacher. I didn't necessarily like that she had a girlfriend—because I was hoping she was waiting for me. But after I met Rusty, things became all right with the three of us. By then—I was older and more mature—in high school.

Rusty had the perfect freckly face. If you could make her laugh, the world was all right and happy. She also had a mean set of arms. She could throw a ball and hit what or who she wanted to hit.

I once sat and watched her throw a softball sixty yards to hit Coach Klekus in the back. When he turned around, she was bent over like an umpire behind home plate and watching the team play. When the ball came rolling back, she picked it up, turned to me, and winked. Her smile was also the mark of the most devious scamp in town.

Rusty was only a small part of my life... but when it came time, and I needed a friendly face in *Stoneheart*, she was there. I needed someone I could hang an extraordinarily complex character on, and still make it the gal next door. I think both Rustys made the world a better place.

I HAD READ science fiction books wrapped in textbook covers all through Mrs. Irvine's seventh grade English class. She drew graphs on the chalkboard the entire year. I read Asimov, Heinlein, Ellison, Norton, and so many others—the entire year.

When I sat down in ninth-grade English, I sat by the back door of the room. By the third day, I would wait until the teacher was deep into her third line of graphs—then slip out the door. I didn't go far. I sat in the hall, where she couldn't see me, but I could watch, or listen to, the teacher across the hall.

I knew Mr. Arnold was teaching an English elective only open to seniors. There were no lines on the board, other than where he had underlined a name to emphasize it as he talked. He talked about writing as if it were alive. He assigned papers like they were water to flow from the students' fountains. The papers were only one or two pages, with subjects as complex as what did you eat this morning, or why is the tree near you so important?

At the end of the second or third week, Mr. Arnold paused in his lecture. He pointed at the window and said, "I want you to write about the window." And then he told the class he would be right back. His hand closed on my shirt collar seconds later, and he backed me out of the other class's door where I had almost made it to safety.

He walked me the short distance out of the building and stood me up against the wall. He held his face a foot from mine. His voice was barely a whisper, and he wasn't threatening me. "Tell me why you're failing your class, but sitting in the hall and listening to mine?"

I wasn't sure myself. "I hate English. It's stupid… all she does is the same stupid diagramming of sentences Mrs. Irvine did in the seventh grade. I hated it then, and I hate it now."

"What did you do then?"

"I read… and almost flunked."

AUTHOR'S NOTE: Many years later, Mrs. Irvine told me I had failed—but I also was doing something the other kids hardly ever did. Read. I was always reading. Even walking the two miles to home, I did it while reading. She was the least surprised I had become a writer. In her words: You can't keep putting information in before some is going to start pouring out.

"But you would rather flunk now… and come into the hall and listen to my class…?"

I nodded.

"You know my class is only offered to seniors, and it's only for advanced placement students." I nodded. "You've listened to the assignments I have given out…?"

"Yes." On my own, I had done the assignments.

"You realize my class is four times harder than her class could ever be?"

"Not if you hate English."

"What do you think it is I'm teaching?"

I smiled. I knew at that moment I had a chance. "The written word… Morning through the eyes of Robert Frost. The cold burning in the marrow of a man's bones long after he stops roaming the Arctic wastelands. The grass between two lovers from the heart of Whitman. You have them writing about a piece of glass right now—not what they see through it… but the glass. The window itself—the object which comes between what we think, what we see, and what we experience."

I rushed on, assured of my position.

"You're not teaching English. You're teaching the written

philosophy of that which is experienced." I smiled weakly and waited. I had hoped I had paraphrased Sartre correctly.

He grabbed my collar again. "Come on." He dragged me back into his class.

The students stopped writing and looked up at Mr. Arnold and his hand grabbing my collar. "Baer knows this class is for seniors. He knows there's daily hard work—but he wants in." He leisurely looked about the class where all the desks were pushed out into a ring around the three walls. In 1966, even the desk alignment was breaking the rules. "This is your class—so you get to vote."

One of the students asked, "What about all the work we've already done?"

"What about it?"

"He would have a week to make up all the work." One of the girls weighed in.

Mr. Arnold turned to the blackboard and wrote: "#1 One week to make up the past work." I already had most of the work done at home. They weren't homework. They were exercises in the creativity of thought put to paper.

He turned. "Anything else?"

"If he misses any homework—he's out."

Mr. Arnold smiled. "Which means if you get sick for a week—and miss a few assignments—you're also out?"

"No... I'm a senior." The statement hung in the air.

Another girl raised her hand. "If anyone misses three papers, they are out. I'd vote for that."

Most of the class was agreeing and nodding. Mr. Arnold wrote it as condition number two—but as a condition for the whole class. The class was taking ownership of making the class theirs.

"Anything else?"

"His work gets graded the same as ours—no exceptions for being younger."

Nobody could think of another condition.

"In Rome, they voted thumbs up or down." Mr. Arnold demonstrated. "If there is one vote of a thumb down… the gladiator died. The same goes here. If you all agree, he must meet the three conditions, and he's in. One vote of no… and he goes back across the hall to a year of graphing sentences."

They all nodded.

"Vote."

I even did the extra-credit papers. I never saw a diagrammed sentence again. It doesn't work for everyone… but I've made it work for the last fifty years.

Louis L'Amour made a living on this same storyline. The young novice is befriended by the older guy, goes against bad odds, wins—but never even gets kissed. He wrote over two hundred books, are all the same story—but told differently. The only difference between Louis and me—I lived this one.

I don't remember what grade I got, but I know it was higher than a D.

BUT, in full disclosure, I've studied and learned more English and about writing proper English in the last twelve years than the previous forty. The biggest lesson was hiring the right editor—the one who spanks my hand, pushes back when I'm wrong, and helps me figure out how to keep my voice as a writer but within the rules.

Much like spelling must conform, your writer's voice can mature, but it must stay true.

You can learn to write like Grisham, Hemingway, or even Railroad Martin, but if it's not your voice, it's just a myna bird or parrot.

WOODSHOP. I took seventeen semesters worth... never got a B once. Mostly mediocre grades because Mr. Kinzy knew I was goofing off and could have done much better work. I hold the record for swats at nine.

I have all ten of my fingers, two working eyes (pretty much), and my hearing. I got my last swat on the last day of classes in the last class (seventh period) in the last ten minutes of the class.

I was the teacher's assistant. The school had never had one before. Mr. Kinzy went to bat for me. He had one every year after.

I was cutting a large block on the band saw. The saw jumped through the last inch in a heartbeat, and my first knuckle on my left hand was in the way. It severed the tendon and cut halfway through the knuckle. For the first second or two, there was no blood. The five freshmen standing around were amazed. Then it started to bleed, and one of them passed out.

I got the swat because it was my responsibility to 1) not show them any blood, and 2) I should have caught him.

The rule was you get to choose your paddle. They were all made from three-quarter clear pine. IF Mr. Kinzy didn't bust the paddle over your butt—you got a shot at him. It had never happened.

I bent over and grabbed my ankles. He wound up and swung. The sound of pieces flying about the shop—didn't happen. I slowly stood up. Kinzy was holding the paddle out to me.

He stepped in and said the secret was 1) never be mad. If you get mad, you won't break the paddle. 2) Aim through the butt and at the head. Swing all the way through.

He handed me the paddle. My hand stopped about where his ear had been. Kinzy was outside the door, dancing around. Just like every other kid with their first swat.

I still have my fingers, eyes, and hearing because Kinzy always cared. The only kid to lose a limb in high school woodshop happened the year after Kinzy and his paddles retired.

I still love working in wood.

Kinzy taught me many things. The one that genuinely stands out was the last—in the last minute of the last class of the year, and my high school career. If you let yourself get mad—you lose.

This lesson is played out in the big fight in *Angel Flights*. If I write it, it will be a pivotal point in the sequel. It is a lesson that bears repeating.

I WAS TAKING Judo and kept muscling and overpowering the other kids. One night the sensa brought a guest. The little girl was his niece. She was eleven or so but looked like she was ready to enter the fifth grade.

Sensa matched me up with her. She dove in and tried for a sweep. I pulled her back... and then picked myself up from the mat.

We bowed, and she walked to the middle. She stood with her arms hanging. I took a stance with my left hand extended. I had no sooner settled into my stance when she slapped my hand. I grabbed for her gee. I pulled her toward me... and found myself flat on my back—with my legs and butt off the mat.

Once more, we met in the middle. I stood as she had. She smiled and then kicked me in the stomach, flipped in the air, and as she landed, she had the collar of my gee. Once again, I was flying through the air.

She was half my size and weight. She was just a little girl. Her uncle told her to now go put on her real belt and help with the class. My instruction was over.

She returned as she put on her black belt. I had underestimated my opponent.

MISANTHROPIC (HATRED of humankind and its nuances), traits in an antagonist or a killer can be as subtle as in a sociopath, or as flagrant as a nasty old hermit. They also make for good pratfalls to bring the character down. But again, there is the antagonist who is merely the thorn in the hero's side—and when something happens, the old bugger can become a confederate.

Not knowing who you are attacking, physically or philosophically, makes great character building.

I had taken algebra as a freshman—it was a requirement. My report card for the four quarters read DFFF. I had to retake it as a sophomore.

We had assigned seats because we had a new teacher. Fresh out of school, Mr. Anderson looked, walked, and talked like Wally Cox, the actor. Being a joke because of his strong likeness was one thing, but driving a VW bug painted primer grayish-brown, with a smokestack coming out of one window—didn't help his image.

By this time, I had reached six-foot and was about one-seventy-five. Humping rocks and firewood for my father had done nothing for our bond, but it had built upper-body strength.

I don't remember who the punk was sitting in front of me, and I'm sure he didn't know anything about me—other than I was dumb enough to have to repeat algebra. He taunted and teased since day one. I ignored him.

Middle of the second week, he placed the large red pencil kindergartners use on my desk. "You dropped your pencil."

Now, by this time, I had gotten to know many of the mentally challenged kids who had been moved over from the grammar school to the high school with their teacher and my friend, Jack Reeder. They were fun and nice and wanted to be friends.

The pencil represented everything ugly they would face in their lives. I could have ignored it—it wasn't really my fight…

Like hell it wasn't…

With my left hand, I grabbed his hair and jerked his head

back and face up as I rose from my seat. My left hand slammed his head back down on my desk.

My right fist came down once, shattering his nose—knocking him out.

As I walked down the hall, Mr. Anderson slid out on his hard-soled shoes. "Where are you going?"

"To the office." I wasn't stupid. I knew the rules.

"See me after school." I turned to see him smiling. His hand was buried in his belly where nobody else could see it—he was giving me the thumbs up.

I never sat in the class again. By an arrangement between Mr. Anderson and Kinzy, I spent the time in the woodshop, turning bowls and gavels. Tuesday and Thursday, after school, Mr. Anderson taught me algebra. I called his home if I was going to be sick or playing hooky. He told me when the tests would be on the desk in the hall. I would stop, take the test, and go play with wood.

The older potential adversary had become my mentor. He understood a lot about being teased, beat-up, harassed, and being the odd one out. I don't know how, but he was the first teacher to make math not so scary. I don't have math anxiety. I have a math phobia. And it blends wonderfully in with the PTSD. Don't make me balance my checkbook—I married my banker for that.

I LEARNED A LOT IN WOODSHOP—LITTLE of it taught to me by Mr. Kinzy. When it came to the lathe, he just pointed to the four lathes. He knew nothing about turning. One of the biggest lessons I learned was someone else's face is more sensitive to the heat of the hot turning tool than my thumb was. I also learned not to touch other people unless invited.

I was in heaven one day. The gouge was throwing the wood,

high over my shoulder, in one long continuous ribbon. I could control where it was going. I loved making it go straight up in front of me about three or four feet above my head... Cutting a clean ribbon is addictive.

One of the younger classmates walked up. He noticed what he thought was smoke or something coming from my thumb. I sensed him standing there and stopped. When he asked if the tool was hot on my thumb, I told him to see for himself. And then I laid the tool up along his cheek. I saw the searing immediately and pulled it off—but the damage had been done. He probably carries the scar to this day. I know it is still seared in my heart.

I've hurt more than a few people in my life—physically. Only a few didn't deserve it. Those few—temper what I write today. They have usually tempered how I have conducted myself since. Okay... advanced years also play into it. But I can still type...

Relationships in small towns are nothing different from in any big city—you just don't have any anonymity in a small town two miles long and the same wide.

During the week and day, Mr. and Mrs. Smith are the scions of the community. They don't have to try to keep up with the Joneses, because they are the same. The same goes for John and Jane Doe. They are good upstanding members of the community, volunteer for this group and that, have the usual two kids, and are square in the middle class. On Saturday night, the TV was limited to the three networks. But there was the movie theater.

When I was fourteen, I was the usher. Now, until then, I believed in the same fantasy everyone else believes about theaters—the lights go down, and you are sitting in a big dark room with everyone else. If you want a surprise, get up in the middle of the next movie you go to. Walk all the way down to the screen, turn and slowly walk back to your seat. Don't worry, you'll find it with ease. You will find it just as if the theater had turned on all the house lights. Believe it or not, it wouldn't be as lit-up as the one huge light down front.

My point is, when the lights go down... you are not in the dark. As the usher, I saw everything. I saw Mr. Smith go sit with Mrs. Jones while Mr. Jones was now with Mrs. Doe while Mr. Doe was sitting with his hand up Mrs. Smith's skirt. Mr. Smith was massaging Mrs. Jones's breast while she was massaging his pants. And so it goes.

The next morning in church, the couples all had the correct partner and were holding their children in check. It was their pious break from stabbing one another in the back on Monday, up and down Main Street, and screwing the other on Saturday night.

Did it make me a cynical curmudgeon? Not. But it did make it easier to leave the church and not take relationships or religiousness at face value.

Over the years, I have learned a "normal marriage" doesn't exist. As much as I would like to believe my sister and middle brother have one—I know there are little differences not expected going in. But if you think I'm calling them out, you couldn't be more wrong.

Their normal isn't my normal. We are different. My brother had three girls and then adopted a handful more. As tight-knit as his family is, at one point, they were spread over three-quarters of the world. Now, it is only half the country and Japan. Now, this sounds normal, but for Americans, it is out of the ordinary. Most of the country never migrates five-hundred miles from where they were born. Some may adopt one or two children, but these two took on a hockey team. Did it work? It does for them—but they aren't Ozzie and Harriet or Ozzy and Sharon Osbourne. But I will say if I were ever to cross the line of writing stories about them and their children—I could fill a fist-full of books. And... I mean in an interestingly good way.

My sister is ranch. Her toes have roots. Her two boys live less than five hundred miles away, and she visits. She cooks, quilts, and births lambs and calves. So, if you are sitting in your apartment in some big city high-rise—don't feel alone. I cook as much as getting food to the table. I do some woodwork. I don't like gardening. And I certainly prefer my cats and dogs to standing in a subzero barn bent over a slimy lamb in January. Also, I'd rather pay my sister to make me a quilt.

Her two sons turned out to be successful as a doctor and lawyer turned judge. But when they were twenty, you could only bet on the one.

When I write about Traumatic Brain Injury (TBI) and Post-traumatic Stress Disorder, I write from my many head shots, my sister's auto accidents, having her face put back together twice, and her husband having a thumbs-worth of frontal lobe removed a split second before the Firestone split-rim flew through the barn roof and landed in the field a quarter-mile away. You want a panel on TBI & PTSD? We're experts. Wait, now that I think about my middle brother flying over his handlebars and landing a hundred and fifty feet away in Tennessee mud—he can be on the panel also. All four of us march to a different symphony or penny-whistle platoon.

What has this to do with my writing? People. Relationships. Family. Anything "normal" is nothing more than a worn-out trope. Ozzie and Harriet Nelson are more the abnormal, with Ricky and Lucy pushing toward the median. It also means anything you can think up isn't even close to stuff out there in real life—so go for it.

In the early 1980s, I sat in a small bar near the University of California at Irvine. My two drinking partners on this fine night was the young woman who had done a midair modern dance earlier in the nude and the guest of honor who we kidnapped.

Well, to be honest, Isaac Asimov was more of an instigating push over. So there we sat, old mutton chops, a closet exhibitionist, and the college disc jockey.

Isaac had wandered into the radio station the day before. My partner and I were recording public service announcements for the lazy disc jockeys to play. The guy with big white mutton chops looked just like the pictures on the back of some of the books I liked to read.

Paul didn't know who the guy was, but I guaranteed him he would have the interview of a lifetime. Every week, we did an interview of the week. One of our two shows was nine to midnight on Friday. We were two goofballs named Clem and Zek. We played obscure country music, but nobody with Junior or New in their name. Hank Williams, but not his son. Riders of the Purple Sage, but not the kids. Any stuff with Minnie Pearl and the Carter family, our groupies, all nineteen of them, couldn't get enough of.

At the stroke of eleven, Paul would start his interview. Often, I was in the other booth doing some goofball voice. It was clean enough for the FCC, but not PC. I would slip him a piece of paper telling him who he was going to interview. We were just having fun. One night it was Bruiser LaRue who had just won the International Truck Off Competition in his pink and lavender custom-painted truck with gold inlaid chrome rims that said, "God Bless John Wayne." The phone, usually stone-cold dead—lit up. Later, the president of the LGBTQ club (or whatever it was in 1981) came up to have a face-to-face with Bruiser and Zek. He knew it was all in fun, and the club usually listened to our show. (We were shocked to find out about the seventeen more fans.)

They had called one another and wanted us to do another interview. Only live. We turned them down but also told him we were touched. We called him the next time we were stuck and going to do a "check-in" with Bruiser. They filled the lobby and

I DRINK COFFEE AND MAKE SHIT UP

did group cheers and other antics. That was the night I found out what a "Furry" was. Go figure.

But, back to Isaac. I worked up about ten questions but didn't give Paul/Zek the sheet with whom he was interviewing until we started. We recorded the whole interview on Thursday night. It ran for two hours instead of the usual fifteen minutes. We recorded the usual goofball stuff leading up. Our friend just had to start the long tape at nine o'clock on Friday night, and then take over our Midnight Madness show, which ran from midnight to three in the morning. We were at the lecture listening to the good doctor.

When I placed the sheet in front of Paul, he read it through. The seven-watt lightbulb suddenly surged to a full two-fifty. We had to cut out the "Holy Shit! Are you really Doctor Asimov?" Paul was a fan of his physics work, but not a science fiction fan. I guess they never put his photo on science white papers. Or Paul didn't pay attention.

It took him a few minutes to settle down, but the interview of Isaac Asimov by the mush-mouthed hillbilly Zek was spectacular and should have made history. But then... KUCI was only pounding the universe with 10-watts of power in those days. And only half of our fan base was listening. Thanks, guys on the swing shift at MacGaw industries. The gay nerds were at the lecture.

So there we three were in the bar. Paul didn't drink but also had come down with something getting in the way of being more than a few seconds from a toilet.

I ASKED Isaac which he found easier to write—scientific white papers or fiction.

His answer made more sense than how we became friends. He said white papers were a process of dumping a bunch of facts and figures into a blender and then pouring them out onto a paper.

Fiction, on the other hand, was tough. You have a story, but it must make sense. Reality and what appears on the news never makes sense. "The guy shot his sister because her husband wanted the shooter's wife, and so the shooter wanted the husband to take her away with him so he could chase his bosses secretary who was having an affair with the boss's wife."

As he said, reality doesn't make a lick of sense. And now you're going to go back to read that mess of sex and lust goulash for the fourth time.

Here is where people who only know me as an adult get to cry foul and cough bull shit—but the reality is what it is.

There are many levels of shyness in the world. There is the quiet wallflower who hardly speaks to people, and then there are the ones who would rather die or runaway than talk to someone new.

I was pretty much both, with a few exceptions. Get me in a classroom with people I have known for years—I could participate. Hell, get me wound up in Pinky Sidebottom's social science class in the eleventh grade, and you couldn't get me to shut up. (There you go, Debbie Mitchell. I said it for you.)

But on a day-to-day basis, I was more comfortable dragging my books from class to class until I could ride away on my motorcycle. I had better conversations while I panted running through the bitterbrush of the sand wash and desert. This is not to say I didn't talk to people; it just means I would have rather not.

The internal conversations go something like this. I see Marilyn. I like Marilyn. I have enjoyed talking to her—okay, listening to her talk. She is a warm, fun person. And I would like to spend some time getting to know her better.

I DRINK COFFEE AND MAKE SHIT UP

Marilyn is fifty feet away, and we are both headed for the front steps of the school. A little sign pops up in my head that says: How about Friday night?

The brain fires up, and this is the internal conversation and decision process:

"What about Friday night?"

"How about the movies?"

"It's Midnight Cowboy. I don't think she would want to sit in the dark watching *that* kind of movie."

"Why not?"

"It's creepy…"

"Then maybe she would need you to hold her hand."

"Grow up."

"What? You have two hands. She has two hands… You two have a lot in common."

"How am I going to pick her up?"

"Get Michaele to drive you."

"Eww… she's my sister…"

"Rather your mom?"

"Don't be a pervert—she was our bus driver. You are such a dork sometimes."

Meanwhile, I am now within eight feet and…

Marilynn smiles and says hi. I wince and grunt. Smooth, cool dude that I am.

Never… even… got off… the bench.

Not getting off the bench is where most people are… for most of our lives. These traumatic internal conversations we had as kids…? Yeah, they were child's play compared with the destruction we perform on ourselves as adults. Nothing has changed; only the stakes are higher as adults.

Nothing has changed—it's still the same dork talking to the other internal dork. It's the driving force in the great movies *Breakfast Club*, as well as *Forest Gump*. In the one, the group bonds to do better, and in Gump, the dork wins despite himself. Either trope, the dork watching or reading wins too. A small seed of winning is planted—and it has us cheering for the dork.

And just to put the polish on the seed of winning—this dork walked down the aisle with Candy McCoy for graduation.

Twice.

ABOUT A YEAR after walking down the aisle with Candy, I worked at a large picture frame shop in Pasadena. My head was still down as I focused on my work. The closest to a customer I ever got was when I had to walk from the back, past the design area, to the only respectably clean toilet. Ninety-nine-point-nine percent of the time, I could pass both ways more invisible than Casper, the friendly ghost. Which was about to change.

Sometime in April or May, I caught some spring crud. It was more than a cold, and I was at home—sick for days. I was bored to tears and looking for something to do. My roommate was gone, so nobody could go to the library and get me more books. So I turned to the phonebook.

Everywhere we had ever lived, there were no other Charlton in the phone book. We moved to Bishop, and there was a Mary Charlton. The phone was disconnected a couple of years before. But now I lived in Los Angeles county. Home to nine million people... surely...

Nope. Two disconnected numbers.

I started looking for names. Vincent Price—not listed. Bela Lugosi—dead and no forwarding listing. Boris Karloff? Evidently, the wrong city. Wait... my longtime heartthrob. Could it be? The spelling of Mae West is unique. Although the prefix was still 213, the phone call from South Pasadena to Hollywood was still a toll charge. I didn't care.

A sweet French voice answered. I croaked out my questions about Mae. Oui, it was the right Mae West, but she was in Paris for the springtime. Yvette must have sensed my letdown. She asked me who I was, and soon, she knew a lot about me, my job, where it was, and why I was home. More importantly, how many of Mae's lines I could recite. The toll charges for that day almost doubled my phone bill. But it was the best medicine ever.

In the early summer, my boss, Norman, stepped around the corner from the front where he had been talking to a customer. He looked the thirty feet back to where I was quietly building frames. Alone.

"Baer?"

I looked up.

He crooked his finger at me. "You have a customer." The three other framers turned to look at me.

Bullshit. I never spoke to customers. I never talked to anyone. I shook my head and returned to focusing on the frame I was making.

He walked back halfway into the workroom. Everyone stopped and watched. He never did such a thing. "If you want a job this afternoon, you will come take care of *YOUR* customer."

I thought about the open door behind me. "I don't do customers. I don't have any customers. That's Clair's and your department."

"You do now. And I strongly suggest you come take care of her before I have to come drag you up front by your collar."

We stood in a standoff. I was almost thirty years his junior, but probably had twice the muscle on him. I put down the finished frame and followed him to the front.

The still classy and gorgeous woman was bookended by two young men who dwarfed me. Their custom shirts looked like their sleeves would burst at any moment. Both had chiseled features and moved like panthers. Her voice hadn't changed in forty years.

"You are Baer, oui?"

I blushed. Even my toes were overheated. "Oui." I stuck my

hand out. "Como…?" I had forgotten any French Mom had taught me, and I was about to start in with Spanish.

She smiled. "It is, *como ta le vu*, Mademoiselle." She extended her hand.

I could feel my face surge from pink to full blood red. She saved me. "We only have to shake."

As my face returned mildly to normal, she said she was flattered when Yvette had told her of the phone call. But it was also fortunate because she had bought a few pieces of art in Paris but had not had them framed.

As we worked on the design, I grew more comfortable. The other three just stood and watched. Her two "companions" I never heard say a single word over the next couple of years. But my boss couldn't contain himself. He cleared his throat at least a few times before he finally just asked. "Are you Mae West, the actress?"

She smiled, and I never forgot her response to blatant adoration. She softly shook her head. "Non, monsieur. Nothing so grand. I am merely a customer of young Baer's."

Let down, he returned to his desk and paperwork. She looked at me with a small coquettish smile and winked. The two walking sides of beef almost smirked. But their eyes were dancing with mirth.

As we finished, and she was leaving, Clair, whose empire I had invaded, was just returning from lunch. As the three walked out, Mae glanced at Clair's large purse and commented something like "nice satchel." The bag was hanging from her elbow with her fingers upright, holding her continual cigarette.

Clair continued ten feet more before her mind engaged. The stunned look on her face was precious. She slowly turned, pointing at the air left by the trio. I had never seen her speechless before. After talking to Norman about the order I had taken, her caustic attitude also became tempered.

The lessons of that day, and the friendship of a lifetime, were never lost. The power of the one phone call changed my life. It changed how or who I talk to. With Norman's constant urging, it created at least a pseudo-extravert. Without the help of a gracious lady, and a couple of great bosses, and a couple of others, I would still be the wallflower in the back of a shop. And… you wouldn't be reading this now.

THE POWER OF PHONE CALLS, or radios for that matter, wend their way through my novels. Phone calls in books can be difficult or even nuisances. Done well, they are seamless and can provide serious impacts. But use them sparingly and wisely.

6

FAMILY

I know. I have already run on about my family. Except, it was only my birth family.

Over the course of a lifetime, the average person will have a few families—let's call her Eve. Yes, like the first Eve.

The four major family groups are: Birth, Collected, Work, and Play Together.

Eve was born into the Smith family. Her Smith family consisted of a mother, father, and five siblings. Within reach of the term "direct family," she had five grandparents, seven uncles, five aunts, and nine cousins. The closest aunt with three cousins lived in the same town, and so they grew up close. Sometimes the two families blended, and the crazy summer bedtime was "who is sleeping at which house." Her best friend was her cousin Betty. Most summers, and weekends, they shared a single bed—cuddled like puppies in their matching pajamas.

The other aunts, uncles, and cousins were as close as a ten-hour drive, to living in a foreign country. She had met most of them at least once at a large family gathering. During college, the daughter of the expatriate family came to visit her. They had been quasi-pen-pals since she had become curious about the "American" family.

In college, Eve lived in the dormitories. By her sophomore year, a group of girls in the dorm decided to apply as a group for the next year's rooming. The seven grew to eleven, and by graduation were what they called themselves the rest of their lives: The Baker's Dozen—thirteen. They worked hard to gather once a year for a "Baker's Weekend."

After Baker College, Eve was accepted into the Navy as a Medic. Because of her grades, the Navy enrolled her in the university to become an MD. She studied hard for eight years and became an expert at thoracic surgery, specializing in explosive crushed bodies. Because of the hidden nature of much of the emergency surgeries, she became recognized for her ability to reach into a body cavity and find a problem where nobody could see it.

It became common for an inbound medivac to call-out that they had one for "Fingers." Eventually, after her saving two bomb diggers and their dog. Her commanding officer presented her with a new name badge. The BDUs were sewn, and her dress uniform was brass. Both were the same—Doc Fingers.

Two tours of duty later, the same officer sat in the courtroom, with tears on his grizzled cheek. The two doctors stood to hear the charges. And were discharged. As they left the building, many who they had worked alongside, saved lives with, got drunk with to fight the horror of war with, and thought of as family… lined the walkway, at attention, and saluted. Being lesbians and loving another woman would continue to be a court-martial offense until it was not.

The two doctors, Eve and Batavia, didn't hold a grudge. They both knew there were rules. They both knew the consequences if they were caught. They were only relieved they could keep their benefits. In defiance, the two walked away, holding hands.

The reaction at home was swift and complete. Eve's mother was hushed on the phone but agreed to meet her at a restaurant about forty miles from home. Eve felt it was one of the sleaziest meetings she had ever arranged. It was the last time she saw her mother before her father's funeral.

Her best friend, attached at the hip since age three, Betty, had summed up her feelings in six words. "You have some nerve calling me." The letters in college had slowed and stopped as Betty had dated and then married the boy and into his church. After hanging up, she hugged Batavia and explained the nature of the church and their beliefs.

Only Eve's youngest brother, based in Italy, had told her at the end of a short conversation, "If you come, I'll take time off, and I can show you around Italy. I miss you, and I will always love you. Bring your girlfriend." It made her want to jump on a plane, with or without a packed bag. Getting used to not having an always packed "Go Bag" was going to take some getting used to.

The two did get on a plane. Batavia's sister met her at the airport. She explained the house had been "strained" since her phone call. The conversation during the drive out into farmland was light but just fluff. Eve was starting to think this had all been a mistake.

The farmhouse was empty and silent. The sister said to go ahead and put their bags in Batavia's old bedroom and come out to the barn. Eve looked questioning at her companion. Batavia only shrugged. It could go either way.

What they could not have expected was the empty barn. A small child stood waiting in the barely opened doors at the other end. He waved and fished his hand for them to come.

As they got close, someone rolled back the large doors to reveal a long table and all of Batavia's family and friends. The balloons were Batavia's favorite colors—purple and gold. The gathering was silent, and then as one, the blended family of

Dutch and Malaysian, all placed their hands together and bowed.

As her mother laughed and summed up their feelings about their relationship. "Who cares? You're dating a doctor. What more could a mother want?"

As the years went by, the two worked in a small rural hospital. Many farming and auto accidents reminded Eve of the damage done by IEDs. Batavia returned to her university to specialize in OBGYN—a specialty always in need in rural areas. They found the small staff of the rural hospital to be accepting, caring, and family. They were invited to all the weddings, celebrated all the births, and attended services in three languages as they paid their respects.

When it became legal for them to celebrate their love and devotion to each other, finally, they celebrated their tenth anniversary with a wedding. The hospital wouldn't let them get married unless it was at the hospital. As it turned out, the only space large enough was the parking lot.

Lines were painted. The high school shop teacher and coach waved his casted arm around as he directed his football and baseball teams how to build the gazebo. Folding chairs from three churches and the two schools were arranged. Everyone laughed that even then, there was not enough seating.

People stood, patients filled every wheelchair and movable gurney, plastic milk crates supported boards, and many farmers backed their pickups and flatbeds up to be filled with bib overalls and square dance dresses. Tiers of hay bales were laughingly called the balcony seats.

The one deputy, left to staff the phones, later reported watching the ceremony on his phone while standing in the middle of the main street. Not even a dog had passed him.

The honeymoon was invaded by the rest of the Baker's Dozen.

Everyone is born into a family—even orphans. This is the family you have no choice about or say in becoming part of. Whether it is a single mom, both parents, or even foster care, it is the first family experience and will influence most for the rest of their lives.

As we get older, usually in our late teens, we begin to form bonds that resemble a family. Time will either dissolve, strengthen, or put on hold those bonds. Some friendships just "mature away." Others become the foundations for standing next to at a wedding. A few fade away, and then there is the wonder of reconnection. The history may have a decade's large gap, but the original bond is all overcoming.

As we settle into working long hours, many find they spend more time with someone at work than their spouse. In recent times, these have become known as the work husband or wife.

I can feel many of you nodding. It is becoming canon.

Even though I have never physically met my editor, when her phone rings later at night, her wife asks if it is her work husband. (Time zones can be a bitch or tell on us). Now the question is just a statement of one or two words. "Baer." Or "your husband." Rogena won't admit whether the giggles still follow.

The hallmark of "maturity" and "creating family" are close. For many, the family you create sometimes happens when someone says, "Yes." It becomes formalized with "I do." But many families formalize with cohabitation.

My hallmark for "maturity," and realizing when you have a family you created, is when a couple stops splitting their time for Christmas. The "your parents for Christmas Eve, and mine for Christmas day," becomes "why don't we just stay here for the holidays." It's a subtle shift. It is realizing and therefore recognizing the new family.

Some will argue the new family is just an absorption into the original family. This might be accurate IF there were only one person with an original family. But even those in foster care usually forge bonds they carry through their lives. So this is more like a new unique family that takes in certain factions of the originals. Even though society views it as getting the whole family as lock, stock, and barrel—the reality is usually not so close.

I gained a brother-in-law when I was about nineteen or twenty. My sister and their boys have been back to Spain and know his family well. Some of his family have come and stayed at their ranch. But I only met an uncle or cousin named Pepe at their wedding. To me, his family are just names. I'm sure they could say the same about me.

My middle brother married an identical twin. And with just that, every spouse of a twin is nodding—they know where this is going. It's the same reality I live with about my wife and the fur children. If it ever came down to the twin or our fur babies, and the spouse—the spouse loses. Every honest twin will tell you the same.

I have also seen this bonding and created family be the breakpoint with marriages and original or blood family. There was a book and a movie about it—*Band of Brothers*.

In boot camp, there were one hundred and ten of us. We lived our lives in one large room. There was a line of toilets along a wall. There was one shower with fifty spray heads. Standing inches apart from another, you stepped into the water, got wet, and stepped out. The bar of soap started at your #2 baby seal haircut and moved rapidly over your arms, body, crotch, and legs. You handed the bar to your partner. As he soaped down, you rubbed over everything once more and stepped in to rinse off. The showers automatically shut off after four minutes. It was expected there was nobody left in the wet area. For ten weeks, everyone knew if you snored, talked in your sleep, or masturbated. If you were caught walking in your sleep, you got a pink slip and were sent home.

Few bonds are formed in boot camp or basic training. But time served on a ship, or in a company, especially in a conflict, can create bonds as tight or tighter than twins on a Vespa in a tornado. Only mutually soiled shorts separate them.

Milder but similar bonds can occur in sports—especially team sports and sports where athlete's careers are over decades. Football, soccer, skiing, and skating come to mind. Some of the runners and those involved in water sports also have one another on speed dial. I guess I also need to mention golf here as well.

I have been graced to write the biography for Jim Taylor, a double amputee. Apart from other pursuits since losing both of his arms when he was ten years old, he golfs. Scratch. Par three. His record is seventeen holes in one. He has a few known names in the golf world on the speed dial of his flip phone. People he has known for more than just a round of golf.

I don't know if I'm becoming part of his family or he mine. It doesn't seem to matter—we both like pancakes, eggs over easy, and bacon.

Family is what I write about. Not Mom, Dad, and the kids—but the other kind. The family you become part of because the caring is mutual. My kind of family. The kind that takes years of caring to build. The kind where birth does not grant instant entry. The type of gene pool some blood doesn't know how to swim in.

If you find yourself drawn to the families in my books, check your family—you might be the same.

7

A TOUGHER EDUCATION – ADULTHOOD, OR ALMOST

So, I got through the twelfth grade—big whoop.

The big whoop was looking in the mirror. I had survived the bully for several years. And then taking seventeen woodshop classes instead of PE and one math class. I was working on my fourth motorcycle. However, I still had both ears, both eyes, the nose broken three times, eight fingers, two thumbs, and ten toes. The braces from the broken jaw were off. And if I didn't shave every morning, I wasn't sent home. Flatly, Helen Welch didn't care if my hair and beard were pink, purple, or gone—only the required white shirt and paper hat for a busboy. The jeans and boots were standard for Bishop.

My eighteenth birthday was still months away when I moved away from home.

Adulthood is when you start learning essential lessons. *If* you pay close attention.

A smart man once said, "The things you learn after you think you know it all—those are the things that count." For a guy who loved wrangling mules in the summer, and less than stellar students all winter, Jack Reeder was a pretty smart fella.

I needed to get down the road about three hundred miles to register for college. I held my thumb out for about twenty minutes. One person stopped and said, "I'm going down as far as the golf course…"

Instead of taking the one-mile lift, I walked the three miles home and changed the oil in my motorcycle. I looked around for my shades and then remembered I had cracked them falling from a cliff. I figured I would buy a cheap pair along the way.

Now, let me tell you the whole story and why it is important to pay attention to things that will become lessons.

Bishop, California, sits on the desert floor of the Owens Valley. If a single puffy cloud shows up between the first of May and the end of September, people run for cover. The air temperature the morning I stuck my thumb out was already in the low nineties. By the time I passed that city limit sign doing fifty, it was closer to hundred-and-five. There are two hundred miles of desert between Bishop and Lancaster. The sort of desert they made movies about. *Death Valley* was only one mountain range over and maybe twenty degrees hotter. (For a better description, read my *Light to Light*. The race was four hundred miles from Mojave to Carson City on 1943 motorcycles.)

In the 1960s, there was a company named Minnesota Woolen Mills. They made great sweatshirts. The best made, in my humble opinion, was the short-sleeved lightweight sweatshirt. The one I wore south was the Navy blue one. Black wouldn't have been any hotter.

Near Olancha, there are the remains of a lake. Los Angeles siphoned off all the water like they did the rest of the valley. The flats are white with pure alkali. August in Olancha can easily reach one-twenty. This stretch of desert is best if you lie on your gas tank and keep the throttle screwed tight to the maximum. A ticket is a ticket, but it beats getting roasted.

The construction lane control reached from Olancha to Long

Lake—twenty miles away. I thought about turning around and going back the mile to the café and wait in the cool with some iced tea. I closed my eyes and dozed until the car behind me honked. The line was moving. Years later, I noticed the café sold cheap plastic wraparound glasses.

As the line crawled at the high-end of first gear and the bottom of second gear, I started to realize how hungry I was. I never liked the food at Little Lake, but Mojave was only an hour away.

The next construction area was forty miles north of Mojave. I never found out why there was an hour delay. It didn't matter. I just leaned into my backpack and closed my eyes. I had learned my lesson—the guy behind me would honk.

I woke up from the noise of people laughing as they drove around me. When I got to the flagger, he took pity on me. He pointed a mile down the highway. "See the white truck with the yellow flashers? You catch up with him, and I'll let you go."

This line of cars was rolling along at a good forty. My bike would do eighty. I passed the truck just before we got to the other end. I had a sandwich in Mojave. I don't remember what it was, but it probably tasted heaven-sent. They didn't have any cheap sunglasses.

About a mile south of Mojave in the heat of the day and desert, the railroad crew had all the traffic stopped as they repaired something with the track. I rode along the side of the highway until I got to a rail person I could talk to. Rails and heat were fascinating. Some of the stories I had heard turned out not to be such tall tales. There was a problem when the temperature is over one-twenty, and they were checking to make sure the rails weren't lifting out of the ballast. Ballast being the rock under the rails and between the wooden ties. By four in the afternoon, we were on our way.

About thirty minutes later, I entered my first freeway. By

seven o'clock, I was booking a room near the Santa Anita racetracks. The woman and man were eyeing my arms and face. The skin blistered everywhere the sun had hit. My eyesight was blurry as well. There was a thick brown line across my eyeballs for years. An ophthalmologist told me I had sunburned the outer layer so badly that it had tattooed the tan line.

I sat in the cool swimming pool for two hours, hopefully sucking the heat out of the sunburn. The woman came to my room with two bottles of alcohol and showed me how to bathe the burn. The third bottle was vinegar to put on once the fever was over. The trick paid off several times during my surfing years.

The next morning, I couldn't see. I had the couple call a friend of mine. Victoria drove me up to the school and did the paperwork. She held two pieces of cardboard for me to sign between. It was the first time I ever knowingly felt helpless. At lunch, she fed me. She stayed for two days until I could see a fuzzy street.

We talked for hours, and then would lay down and nap. We talked about growing up in a small town where everyone knows you—or thinks they do. Years later, I sat through the *Breakfast Club* from the early show to the end of the last show. There was a bond there.

We discussed being ignored. People thought I was stuck-up. Victoria knew it was because I was shy and afraid of people. She had sat in front of me in our anthropology class. I was in love with her long straight hair and the long fringe of her leather jacket. I made a quiet comment one day about braiding the two. We had dated a few times before school ended. The most we ever did was kiss.

She told me about growing up in a redneck cowboy town and being only one of a few lesbians. She had dated me because she knew I was friends with the three gay guys in town. She figured I was safe. I think she took my hand first.

I DRINK COFFEE AND MAKE SHIT UP

That week I learned about being afraid. Being afraid of nothing can sometimes be more paralyzing than knowing the dangers of who you are and moving forward anyway. It would take a couple of great bosses to show me how to swim in the deep end of socializing, but Victoria showed me strength in the face of real danger. Those were still the days when people were brutalized and killed for being different—male or female, black, brown, yellow, or pink. I can never forget her and her compassion of those days. And the fear she let me in to see, which had become her strength. If there was ever a role model for the character Blake in my *Pirate's Patch*, it was Victoria. I think she would blush to be told it, but she should be proud.

Someone once thought they were writing a snarky review of one of my books. They wrote: "He shapes characters that are more openly giving and caring than reality. He writes about events that make a great fantasy, but people just are not that gushy kind and giving. Mr. Charlton needs to grow up and join the twenty-first century."

I asked the reviewer if she had ever heard of Make a Wish Foundation, Dads for Kids in Chairs, Paying it Forward, Random Acts of Kindness…? They had… but had never witnessed or heard of anyone receiving such foolishness. I wept at the fact she was fifty-eight, and nobody had ever just done something randomly kind for her.

I thought long and hard about her heart chilling and hardening. I didn't want to know about her rapport with her husband or three kids. It didn't matter. I sent her a bouquet of two-dozen daisies. The card was the hard part to make. It simply read: "Happy Dr. Seuss Day."

As we get older, the stories don't get longer—they just become more complex.

When we were kids, chicken noodle soup could come out of a red and white can. It was chicken stock, salt, egg noodles, salt, and itty-bitty chunks of salty chicken. We didn't care about the salt, or what it did to our blood pressure, or if it shortened our lifespan. What we did take away from a bowl of hot chicken noodle soup was the salty crackers, a warm tummy, and someone made it for us. The lessons were simple and pure.

As we got older, we began to worry about the salt. The chicken stock we examined for antibiotics and other hormones. The chicken became a bone of debate next—is it organic or worse, is it vegan fed. Next, we will want the can to be marked with what state it was canned in, or if the paper label from recycled paper?

Things got complicated, but sometimes plainly simple.

WHEN I WAS TWENTY, I was living in a small two-bedroom house in East Los Angeles. The house was in a quiet older neighborhood. Well, most of the time. I loved my time there enough to put the house and my roommate in a book—whole cloth.

If you have read *Angel Flights*, the house, the house rules, and everything about Gertie was my life. I got home one night and realized the lawn was almost ankle deep. I didn't think about the hour. The coffee was on in the kitchen, the light over the sink was on, and there was no lock on the back door.

I got the reel lawnmower out of the garage and started pushing it about the front yard. As I was finishing, the night became day. The two cops got out of the cruiser but left the spotlight on me. I guess a large dude in surf baggies and a lawnmower was a strange sight at one in the morning.

They watched as I mowed the last two passes and followed me to the garage. They oohed and awed over my chopper and made points. We sat in the kitchen and talked for about an hour.

Two more cops knocked on the open front door. I made more coffee. By sunrise, the butt-sniffing was complete. The coffeepot was rarely turned off—it just got replaced by the large church-sized coffeemaker.

Gertie, my fourteen-foot boa constrictor, came into my life about a month later. The barbeque pit got build the next summer, and the fridge always had frozen steaks in it. Life was simple, if not just a little unusual.

My friendships, in my mind, were simple. I prized my quiet, and the cops prized a safe place to relax and do paperwork, and coffee they didn't have to shell out nickels or dimes for. After a while, they got used to Gertie and she to them.

But if you start to break down the relationships of cops to a biker, a biker who painted, a biker who had an aggressively lesbian snake larger than most men, and a snake who loved the smell and feel of fresh-mowed lawn and the touch of a dozen little kids hands on her slippery skin—things start getting very strange and complicated. But hey, we were all adults—except the neighborhood kids.

EARLY IN MY ADULTHOOD, I had gotten a phone. It was on the nightstand next to my bed. One night the phone rang. I opened one eye. The flip-number clock showed 2:36 in the morning. I thought it had to be a wrong number dialed by a drunk. I rolled over and ignored the next twelve rings.

Four days later, I was a pallbearer at his funeral.

Always answer the phone in the middle of the night. If it's a wrong number, make sure they are all right, and then you can go back to your safe sleeping. If it is a friend who needs to talk or needs your help... be *THAT* friend who was worth reaching out to.

We had never heard about PTSD in those days. Few had ever

even used the term "flashbacks" about their experiences in Vietnam. "Shell shock" was the shatter pated state of the old guy who never mentally came home from World War II.

Boy, did we have a lot to learn... and many funerals to go to.

From that funeral on, the phone was by my bed, and I always answered it. I would like to say it was out of compassion, but it was also out of my own selfish needs. I would rather have my night interrupted than go to a funeral.

The opening scene of *Angel Flights* comes from just such a night. The circumstances of our knowing each other were different, but the result was the same. The young woman became Gertie's new bed buddy for a while, and I had my whole bed to myself for a couple of months. She finally worked things out with her parents and moved to San Diego State and a dorm. And then I remembered what it was like to sleep in a double bed with a snake who could rearrange you in the bed. By then, Gertie was well over a hundred pounds. Dealing with a snake half your weight, but ten-times your concentrated strength, is an incredibly humbling experience.

The phone on my nightstand also led to the cell phone in *Stoneheart*. Our ability to reach out, across the street or thousands of miles, is the ability to connect us. It also can estrange relationships. "I'll call them later, or tomorrow..." all too often becomes weeks or even years. In our busy lives, time slips away.

One weekend, I had arm-wrestled to the semi-finals in front of a large crowd. Even after I lost, I had shaken hands, stood, and puffed out my sixty-eight-inch chest to stretch the oversized tank top. My twenty-three-inch biceps engorged and hot. They looked like two hanging Italian hams. I adjusted my thirty-one-inch belt to hang better on my six-pack and strutted slowly off the stage.

The next morning, I stared at the gray-haired man in the mirror and wondered what the hell had happened. Rip Van

Winkle has nothing on us. Life sneaks up and steals years from us—catching us all by surprise. The sixty-year-old who says otherwise—is a liar.

Nobody is exempt. Age surprise always rings true. That's what makes it such a powerful tool in telling stories—older people nod their heads and relate. One of my bosses, who was well into his eighties, told me he was only twenty-three. His only problem was his mind kept writing checks his body could no longer cash.

ITCHY FEET. Wanderlust. The need to see the other side of the mountain. The burning need to cross the big muddy. A goal to stick your feet in the water of a different ocean. The ache between the shoulders to hike a new mountain range, paddle on a strange lake or river you have only read about—this is what drove Lewis and Clark to the Pacific. Few have ever said, "The ten blocks of my neighborhood are enough."

I dated a woman who had only been to the edges of California, and never to the northern half. The idea of going "beyond" filled her with wonder, but also fears of the unknown. I eventually took her to Hawaii. I could tell she was right up against the outer edge of her comfort zone—being in that *foreign* land.

We ate at McDonald's, California Pizza, Denny's—just like home. I understood. Eventually, we went to a luau. She was fine. The beach reminded her of one near home. I had to admit the sand felt the same, people looked the same, and the sun even went down the same. We were just three thousand miles further out onto the Pacific Ocean.

Perception is what can give us refuge in a strange and scary place or situation. It is the reason hospitals no longer paint their walls Eisenhower green. The number one selling house paint is

Navajo white, also known as antique white. Hospitals found people to be more comforted by the color they associated with home.

When I was a stringy youth, I rode my motorcycle out of the state I grew up in. I took off across the desert of Nevada. My story would have possibly ended there, but I was with a friend. Jack was on his Honda 750. He would be with me until Colorado, and then he would turn south to visit family in New Mexico. Luckily, he was still there in Nevada as I dozed off, staring at the next hour of straight highway. He honked his tinny horn and screamed at me to wake up.

A while later, we sat in the shade of a small gas station reeking of bad sewage, scorched grease, and spilled diesel fuel. The only shade was on the bathroom side of the building. The hard-beaten dirt parking lot where our bikes stood is probably still a toxic superfund site.

It was my first experience with a grape Nehi. Probably my last.

The soda was sickly sweet. The long red needle of the large round thermometer in the office bent buried well past the last tick marked—120°. We filled the canteens with the questionable brown-tinged water and pushed on.

Ely, Nevada, was a little cooler after the sun went down. We rolled out just our ponchos and lay sweating on the brown grass of the park. The next night would have us waxing fondly of the heat, stars, and smell of scorched lawn.

Never camp on the shores of the Great Salt Lake. The Utah mosquito has a stinger capable of penetrating jeans, sleeping bags, and probably armor-plate steel. In the dark, we pitched our tent, slapped at mosquitos, rolled out our sleeping bags, slapped and slapped, and… threw our gear on our bikes, and ran like hell.

We didn't want to spend the twelve dollars for the room, but the shower was probably appreciated by those around us in the next few days.

THE KINDNESS OF OTHERS:

I had left Oklahoma City shortly after midnight. The light drizzle was joined by lightning and thunder made louder by the closeness on the open plains. You don't have to worry if the flash is a few seconds before the boom. It is when the black air turns stadium bright, and the bolt of lightning strikes the top end of the trailer in front of you as the thunderclap deafens you.

I huddled under the next overpass, staring at my motorcycle.

After about an hour, I was wondering if the rain would stop and where the next off-ramp with something for cover was.

I don't remember the trucker's name. He stopped, and I told him why I was hiding. He never laughed. I followed him to the truck stop about twenty miles up the road. He bought me breakfast. We talked about life on the road in a truck vs. motorcycle. Working instead of just traveling. California and the Midwest.

Finally, I asked him why he stopped. I asked him why he not only stopped but then bought me breakfast. A biker he didn't know.

It was hard for the man not to start bawling. About three years before, his boy came home from Vietnam. It was hard for him to settle back into the old job or even the house. One day, things blew up. They had words. His son packed a bag, strapped it to his motorcycle, and then left. He hadn't heard a word from his boy since.

The last words they had were harsh.

The man was in hell. I could see and feel that. Since then, I have wondered if the son and father ever reconnected. There is an ulcer in my soul from where the question wears. I believe in the universe. I believe the universe can and will take care of you.

So I put a cure out there in the universe… I hope it worked as well for them as it did on me. The names Slim and Oceal are only placeholders for all of those who can use a little healing.

Isaac Asimov once told me there was a small part of being a compelling fiction writer. It was being god. You can create whole galaxies, expand to universes, or just create a character. You can make them any way you want. You choose.

They can be happy, or at a whim, you can toss them in the stormy seas of desperation or dash them on the rocks of despair. You decide everything about them, or little and let them grow within their dialogue and the reader's mind. You are god.

But the truth is—we get to build the foundations. Some days it is like you just raised a child, and they took their first step. In the third step, they took as a fully realized adult character. As you sit backscratching your head and wondering at what happened… they take control of the story, and your life is never the same again.

A couple of years ago, several writers were having lunch at a convention called Murder and Mayhem in Milwaukee. Wisconsin is a central location, and we were from all over the states.

We went around the large table, describing how we built stories and characters. Some were extreme plotters who work out every single tiny detail. I remember wondering if one writer just threw another five thousand words at the detailed outline and called it good. I have since read two of her books, and I still wonder about that.

One person was a short story writer. As he explained how he got his ideas, his wife quietly sat there, nodding her head, confirming it was all true. She taped up various pages of trashy supermarket check stand sleaze papers. With a blindfold in place, he threw three darts at the wall covered with these papers. Where the darts hit the header or the picture, no matter the page—it was the basis for his next story. If it hit a name, it was the main character. Any mention of a city or location became the setting.

When it finally got to the bottom of the table, and me—it was getting late. One of the other writers had read a few of my books and chuckled something to the effect about *This ought to be good...*

I admitted to building my characters with depth. Not on paper, but in my mind and dreams. I usually had a foundation worked out about the story in my head. "So, I get all the characters into the room, sit them down, and explain what the story is, how it will progress, and the ending we are driving toward..."

There was silence until John said, "And...?"

I stood. "Well, after the laughing calms down, they sit me down, tie me to the chair, duct tape my mouth shut, and explain what I need to write for chapter one..."

The next panel was being introduced when we burst into laughter. We seriously tried hard to be quiet. If anyone took offense that year—I'm sorry.

YES, I realize I'm jumping around here. Adult education strangely works that way. Once you leave the pedagogical progression of school—lessons and tests don't come in any logical progression.

I've told one of my editors this for years. Specifically, I told Mar Penner Griswold, if I put something in a book and describe it so you could pick it up and recognize it, or a character—it or they are almost never a throwaway. I'm sure she is still waiting for me to get back to a gas pump jockey named John. She raised holy cane with me because there was already another John in the book.

I explained to her about the facts of life. There are no less than forty-three Johns in my cell phone. I regularly interact with three every week who are not in my phone. John is a common name. So is Mary. Or Maria… My mother's name was Ruth. Her mother's name was Ruth. But for clarity, I renamed one John to be known as "the Squirt." But just to give her conniptions, I snuck another John in here and there. It's how life works sometimes.

8

LET'S TALK ABOUT DEATH

If a small drop of ice water just ran down your spine—this is why.

We are affected by five different forms of death. I'm not talking about the difference between cancer and getting hit by a car... but just simply death—of other people around us.

- First is the distant. This is the stuff we see on the news. Rarely are the deaths we see someone or people we personally know. We deal with the horror much the same way we handle death in a movie. We are passive observers. Sometimes we record the evening news so that we can speed through the "who shot who" and the day's death toll.
- Next, we know the person but are more associates than friends. They may be someone in your church or down the hall at work. But you have never cracked a beer with them. Nor would you ever. This is more the "familial distant." They are detached from you and your life, but you are familiar with them. More than likely, they are more a friend of a friend. So, when

your friend is impacted and gets weepy—this is when you remember you have a root canal or need to get a big job out before the boss fires you. In a way, this makes it creepily squirmy by association. (Easy to write about to make readers squirm.)
- The circle of friends comes next. These are people you have had the beer with. You served or work with them. You had barbecues together. These are the ones you first learned to hug, pee-pee to pee-pee or boob to boob—the ones who, in tough times, you could hang on and just cry together. Macho or Sista, it didn't matter—you were there for each other.

This is the point where death starts getting real. This is the level where you take a seat when you hear. You try to explain, and then just fan your hand and head for the bathroom. Maybe you make it to a stall, and perhaps you don't. If you end jammed against the wall, or maybe slump to the floor—it just doesn't matter—you don't care. Your guts are churning or knotted. What you had for lunch might not be around for dinner. Your head is frozen at the sound of the words and is also a vacuum with no place to move to. The body goes numb, the muscles are sponge with no strength, and you give in to the loud gray static of the void.

This is the place most writers write from. This is the aching silent scream, the tortured face, the undying death. But this is where Hollywood and most writers draw the line. The last—is too personal.

- This is the place where your mother's eighteen months—dancing with cancer—lives after she dies. The whole ball of fungible fecal festivities slowly rolls around in this purgatory, which prevails while she is there, and then persists for long periods post morning.

> This is the hell which comes thirty or more years later when you are telling even a happy story… and your voice cracks, your throat swells, and the frog croaking from deep in the loss is the only sound. This is the place, which is so unique, it defies description, and yet —it is almost universal.

Okay, that description was for my mother. Or at least the memory of her. The mother I set type with and spent thousands of hours printing cards and money with would be the first to forgive my true feelings. The most fucked up shitstorm of the feelings to hit the searing back of the throat. Until you get there, don't ever try to tell someone you know how they feel. This is where the fellowship gets small and real.

Sorry, but that "sorry for your loss" shit… Fuck you. Don't ever say that to ANYONE. Only a stupid cop on TV says something so stupid. You aren't sorry because you didn't know the person. And as for the "loss"—you have no fucking idea. So just nod your head and get back in your stupid car.

BY THE WAY, if this gets too uncomfortable—kick it forward a bunch of pages and find the picture of the kittens. This is going to take a while, but we'll catch up with you.

No, there isn't a picture of kittens, but they'll figure it out and be back… or go sell their copy of this book at a used bookstore.

Harsh? Yeah, a bit. But death is something people weird out about. And yet, the experience is universal. Not just our own, but in all formats. Death, like having babies, is the endcaps of life.

Surrender to its existence, and you will be more comfortable with the crap between birth and death.

If you can't handle it in reality—you sure as shit won't do well writing about it. In fact, if death is too much... life is not your schtick either. So don't write long-form. Try event writing instead. You can't write about living without the influence of the other. As we get older, the nearing of our death and observance of those close to us drives us to make bucket lists. We go see places or see relatives we would never have before. It's part of putting our house in order.

It's a powerful motivator.

When I sat down to write *Angel Flights*, my good friend Rabbit had until spring. When the pain was too much for the painkillers, he went back down to Mexico for one last memorable sunset and then adios—but he wanted to see it written first. I was 36-days away from having what turned into an extensive surgery on my right shoulder and back. I typed "the end" on 148,000 words just after midnight before surgery.

I checked my email before I left for the hospital.

The note from Rabbit read: "I like how it ended. A lot."

Ninety-three days later, he left a note and a thousand dollars for his burial under the beer bottle. The note just said to bury him and to call me.

IN THE SEVENTH GRADE, there was a kid named Dave. He had a wad of dark hair over a chiseled face. For me, the stand-out was him being a genuinely nice guy. I remembered him squatting down next to one of the mentally challenged girls. She didn't have any money for ice cream after lunch. He asked if she liked ice cream. She had only nodded. He reached in his pocket and pulled out some napkins. (First... what eleven-year-old boy even thinks to get napkins, much less use them?)

He passed her some and helped her spread them out on her lap. He then took his ice cream sandwich and broke it in half. I had noticed he gave her the larger part. She was probably three or four years younger than us, and about half his size. He might have been six-foot by then but seemed larger.

They sat there eating the ice cream in silence. The ice cream was the excuse; he was there to sit with her. She always sat in the same spot to watch the four-square game, which nobody invited her to play. When she finished, he helped her clean up her hands... and after she said thank you... he kept sitting until the bell rang. They didn't talk. They didn't need to. Sometimes just sitting quietly with someone is enough.

Summer and swimming come to the Owens Valley by the first of May. A few weeks before school got out, Dave and another boy had gone down to the river. Many of us kids did. If you had a bicycle, it was only a half-hour ride.

One of the things about growing up country is learning what you can eat growing wild in front of you. I've always felt bad about the many Snow Flower plants I found and ate. The term "endangered" wasn't a word most kids understand.

The leafy plant named water chestnut looks a lot like Italian parsley. Both are tasty and edible. Hemlock also grows along the river. It is only slightly bitter and smells like burnt almonds mixed with burning rubber. But in the hot sunshine... you can't smell the warning scent.

School was let out to attend Dave's funeral.

For some, the abstract idea of one of us dying was too much. It was just a day to go sit on the lawn and wait for the bus to take them home. I don't remember if I went to the funeral or sat on the lawn. But I do know I have never thought about Dave... without thinking about the little girl in the red dress, sitting in the shade eating ice cream, next to Dave... like they were friends.

Dave was well-liked—popular even—but I don't remember him ever hanging with anyone else.

The first dead body I ever saw not in a coffin, was when I was twenty-one. The seventeen-year-old was in my driveway.

A cop, who was a friend, stood there with me in the driveway. He kept asking if I was all right. I didn't move—or talk. I was processing the idea of a dead body. But also, one that was in my driveway.

Later, they had the paramedic give me a shot of something. He said it would help me sleep. I remember him getting scared and backing up into the wad of cops in the door to my bedroom. Gertie, my hundred and twenty-pound snake, had decided it was time to make the others go away. She stacked on the bed behind me. At sixteen feet long, her head was inches from the ceiling—poised as if to strike. They left, and she oozed down on top of me, and we slept the clock around. No one spoke of the night again. The back door still didn't have a lock when I moved out a year later. I always wondered what it must have been like for the poor next tenants—cops walking into the kitchen night and day.

When I was driving a tow truck on the south side of San Jose, three incidences solidified my beliefs about the randomness of death. People being assholes when they don't consider others. And people being mega assholes when they don't think.

If you have read my Southside Hooker series, you know the story about the prom queen. But there were two girls, two separate accidents, and I married them together.

The red truck was the first. The story of the accident under the Alters, I took the whole cloth. There are some events you just can't make up—especially accidents.

For those who haven't read the series, here is the story.

. . .

I DRINK COFFEE AND MAKE SHIT UP

It was one of those freak October nights when the humidity from the bay meets the cold air pushed over the Santa Cruz mountains. It wasn't enough to even call a rain, but drivers react to what is on their front window long before the squirm of their tires. Most had ignored the thin layer of wetting on the summer's built-up oil on the southbound 101 freeway.

In the prosperous times under Governor Reagan, many highway construction projects had been started. A large and high "Los Angeles" style interchange of the three freeways of 101, 280, and 680 had begun construction. First raised were the overpassing exchange stands. Then another election cycle had swept the new junior Jerry Brown into office. The very large infrastructure war chest had evaporated in a matter of weeks. The "shrine" to "Moonbeam" Brown was a stack of two four-lane transitions, one on top of the other. Hovering thirty feet above the 101, where the 280 would become the 680, was a northbound 101 transition overpass to northbound 280 capping it all forty feet higher.

Besides being the butt of every joke known to transportation about being an "altar, still looking for a virgin to sacrifice," the structures were also the source for many wrecks on the 101. Some involved gawkers or the occasional idiot who tried to take a picture while driving, but more wrecks happened as the dangerous rain season started.

Under the stacked altars, the surface is protected. So the oil that builds up throughout the summer is the last to dissipate or get washed away. Specifically, on that fateful night, the already wet tires of many cars ran over the oil at speed and started slipping. Emerging from the underpass onto the truly slick entertainment field of four lanes of water over oil, the hydroplaning tires never stood a chance. What should have been an orderly progression of cars ended up looking more like a yard sale on a late Saturday afternoon. Seven tow trucks were called for seven cars, and by the time they arrived, there were fourteen to be towed.

Hooker hadn't been called out but had merely been returning to his territory when he saw the mess. A tall CHP officer had been standing along the side and waved him over and pointed at a creative cluster that may have started as three or four cars but was by then just a mass of mangled colored steel and rubber. Not knowing what else to do, and not having been called out, he began sweeping the traffic lanes while the other drivers hooked up in a ceaseless leapfrog of blow-and-go. As things cleared out, and his pail got heavier, Hooker just dumped it in the others' pails and kept sweeping. His service in the wet, cold dark night was not going unnoticed.

Mike had been one of the older and more observant drivers brought down from up north. He had stashed two cars in a parking lot within a mile and was hooking up his third as he slipped Hooker the keys to an AMC Pacer and told him where it was. It was a "dead bone" or worthless, but it was at least a tow.

But as Hooker was pulling out, so the Chip could clear the scene, he noticed a red 1952 Chevy pickup with baby-moon hubcaps and an expensive paint job. The truck was over in the shoulder, facing up the small berm, and didn't seem to be part of the massacre. Hooker had watched the red truck as his wipers clacked an ominous counting of time, and time suspended. Something about the truck tied itself to Hooker, and he felt it was worth pointing out to the officer; and who knew, he might even give the tow to the kid.

The officer had told Hooker to go over and check it out to see if it was part of the night's mess, or if someone had just parked a break-down at a strange angle. As Micha cleared the traffic, he was only seconds behind when Hooker opened the driver's side door.

As Hooker approached the truck, he saw an occupant, a young blonde. She was the kind of girl any red-blooded American boy with a pulse would have been proud to take to the prom and who, he later discovered, had been the prom queen just the year before. She turned her face toward him. "Are you all right?" he asked as he reached over and opened the door.

The gorgeous beauty blinked her powder-blue eyes once and then slumped out of the truck and into Hooker's arms. He barely caught her as she sighed and said, "Don't let me die." And then, she was gone.

Stunned, neither Hooker nor Micha moved. It was all just too overwhelmingly surreal for either to think about performing CPR. The wet turned to rain as the two soaked men stood on the side of the highway, washed in the red and blue flashing lights and wept. It would be many minutes before the last paramedic came to check on the two standing off in a dark corner. Nothing was ever really said after that, but the two men knew they shared a commonality far beyond anything they could ever say to each other.

Several years later, Micha had bought Hooker a shot of whiskey in the bar at the Bold Knight on Monterey Highway. Hooker didn't understand the unwarranted gesture until the man had clicked their two shot glasses and said quietly, "Here is to beauty queens in pickup trucks, may they always be remembered for their laughs, smiles and the way they make their daddies proud; and may there always be many more."

THE OTHER PROM queen was later and in the spring.

The deadly curves south of Calero Dam are real. In fact, just about all the streets, roads, and places I write about in the Hooker series are or were real. The curves... were very deadly.

I got a call just before the gray light of morning. A local had called in a wreck. The sheriff station was sending up an officer. When I arrived, right before the state fire truck and two CHP officers, I understood. The car was upside down. When it was new, it had been a Triumph TR-6 convertible sports car. Even with its tires reaching for heaven, it was a sexy car. The sheriff's deputy even smirked about how it looked like his date the week before: "Legs in the air, yelling oh God, I'm coming."

We chuckled, but nobody had remembered the doughnuts, so I went to work rolling the car over.

I felt the engine, and it was long cold. It had probably flipped sometime shortly after midnight. I looked at which side was the most torn up. I knew I would crush it even worse as it rolled. The side facing the hill was the battered upside. We figured it had spun and rolled at the same time. The top was toast, so it didn't matter. So I ran the line around and hooked it into the shattered front light.

The truck didn't even strain as I spun the car around. The squealing metal in the early morning air was like fingernails on a chalkboard. None of us wanted to listen.

As I set my small hooks into the manufacturer's tie-down slots, the deputy walked up. From the look on his face, the news wasn't going to be good. It turned out he had run the plates. The car belonged to one of the larger homes about a mile further south. The substation had made the call. The owner said his daughter had the car and was at her girlfriend's house. The daughter had been elected prom queen, and as a reward, he had let her use the car.

The man drove up a few minutes later. The fuzzy slippers were a nice touch. The pajamas with hundreds of little purple hearts on them were too much to look at. It was something even Willie would have drawn the line at wearing—much less be seen in public. He stood there as I rolled the car.

We could have never told him what to expect. None of us wanted to be there at that moment.

When a convertible does a header, the body left is only intact from about the armpits down. The head is usually popped off and in the backseat. Occasionally, they get ground off. Every accident is a crapshoot. We had been standing around the car for an hour. I had spun the car with ear-shattering noise—yet we heard nothing. The half-dozen of us professionals knew what we would find.

With the daddy standing watch, I decided to forgo the slow, careful roll. I lifted the two levers and brought it over. The car body came up on edge, hovered, and then crashed down. The car rocked on the four tires and shocks. The silence was deafening.

Suddenly, a head of mussed blond hair popped up. The eyes had a cheerful wildness to them that matched the squeaky spunky voice. Her breath still smelled like a turned-out brewery.

"Good morning! Hi, Daddy. Oh… hi, Daddy…" Her voice faded off.

The man and his political power were known to many of us.

Everyone, except the original deputy and I, suddenly had places to go. The man grabbed one of the paramedics and growled something about making sure she was not dead. We were certain it wouldn't be long before she wished she were—prom queen or not.

THE NEXT STRAWS on the camel's back were three accidents on Blood Alley. I described the bloodiest ten miles in US history in the books. I'm sure I haven't even gotten close to why it got its name.

Sit in a parking lot some time. Make sure you back into the space. Look at your door mirrors. Now, look at the mirror of the guy next to you. Carefully notice how many inches away from each other you are. Now imagine you and the other car are both driving at fifty-miles-an-hour. Now imagine the other guy is a tractor-trailer-trailer. Now imagine the guy driving the big rig has been driving sixteen or eighteen hours a day for the entire week. *That* is Blood Alley.

When IBM let go hundreds of engineers, more than enough looked at the oncoming truck and swerved into the truck's front grill. Most of the engineers were driving small light cars such as VWs, Toyota Corollas, Gremlins, or the AMC Pacer. A call-out to Blood Alley usually meant you would end your shift there. Bring the snow shovel, mop, and extra bags of sand.

Unfortunately, my shift never ended. I was the contract driver. My shift for the entire south end of San Jose (487 square miles) was on-call 24/7. A late afternoon call-out could likely run until a break long enough to breathe in dinner. Dessert could be a jumpstart or a flat tire. This gets washed down with a squawk on the shop radio, a fast refill of ten gallons of sand, dump the glass bucket, check the flares, and turn on the yellow rotors. The north end of Blood Alley was only a mile from my house.

It took California many years to build a barrier wall. I never mourned for the engineers. I finally quit towing because of the collateral lives, as well as the family of the cowardly jerk who crossed the line of yellow paint.

THE NINETEEN EIGHTIES brought us seemingly a land rush for cemetery plots. By 1984, I began to think of Saturday being a day driving somewhere, and then standing by a grave in a black sport coat. It was an era that, deep in my soul, I wish had never happened.

I buried vets who had returned from Vietnam, only to find Vietnam had not stayed there. Most suffered from PTSD, but of course, the VA and Army said it was just all in their mind. Others were already dealing with the aftereffects from exposure to Dow Chemical and Monsanto's wonderful contribution to the war effort—Agent Orange (the forerunner to Round-Up and the rise in cancers in the United States).

The industry of professional picture framers, as well as the adjunct industry of interior designers, decorators, and artists, was full of the first wave of AIDS-infected. There were Saturdays with coordinated funerals.

One such day, three services were held back to back at Forest Lawn. The saddest part of those funerals were the families who refused to accept the men's sexuality. The three men had been friends. They had bonded strongly during their battle. One of their partners later told me they had wanted to be buried together if it was possible. One was buried in a closed casket. The other two were cremated and placed in the grand mausoleum. Ignorance, prejudice, and denial ruled the day. From then on, I have made it crystal clear about my eventual shake and bake ashes to be spread somewhere at sea.

9

CHRISTMAS

As I said before, Christmas isn't one of my happy times. Sometimes I get the follow-up question—"Didn't I ever have a good Christmas experience?"

The answer is sure—but you won't like the story.

As I said before, my mother was psychic. And then she was a born-again Christian. The church told her that her "second sight" was the workings of the devil. No proof, just something someone thought up. A blanket statement of faith that denied every mother's intuition about their children: and this is where my sister will close the book and set it aside to maybe throw away later. We still have our differences in beliefs. For me, I inherited some of my mother's insight. So here is my "Best Christmas."

Christmas was never a big thing with me. More often than not, wrapping hand-me-down boots and mended socks just seemed somehow wrong. So, getting old enough to be on my own made it a lot better.

In Southern California, after closing the shop Christmas Eve, I would have a quiet dinner with my Jewish boss and go home. Later, I would wax my surfboard, then sleep until almost dawn

I DRINK COFFEE AND MAKE SHIT UP

and head for the surf. Christmas was quietly in my own space, with others, on the water. More than not, the water was flat. We were there—to not be elsewhere.

But if I were to choose the best "Christmas," it would have to be the year I blew the motor on my motorcycle, so I was taking the bus everywhere. I had stopped surfing, so there was nothing to look forward to…

About eight p.m., I was riding the bus past the Greyhound station. I saw a bus sitting in the bay that said Reno. I got off the metro bus and bought a ticket home to Bishop.

The folks lived about eleven miles north of town. I talked the driver into dropping me at the bottom of the hill. He was a little sad because only one other person was going on farther that Christmas Eve. As the diesel fumes hung in the three-a.m. air, I looked across the valley at the Sierra Mountains, and especially Mt. Tom.

The stars don't "wheel" overhead. They just hang like a breath caught in surprise. The crisp night was turning my lips blue, my ears red and causing my nose to run, but I don't remember or nor did I care. The moon was just up for about two or three hours and flooded the valley floor. The snow-blanketed mountains glowed with the soft brilliance only coming from a quarter moon.

The road's gravel crunched in frozen protest to my boots as I walked up the hill. It's less than a half-mile, but I always made the hike last. The desert calm on a windless night in the frozen winter is a vision of ghostly sound. You know there should be movement or the sound of a far-off truck. But the only sound is your heart beating. The lighter grays on the darker blacks are all waiting for you to pass on into the rest of the night.

As I got to the midpoint of the driveway and near the back gate, I stopped and turned to just rest and stare at the snow folded in the valleys of the mountains. The knees of the ridges cutting dark, jagged knife tracks down the slopes I had hiked and climbed as a kid. Now, they were bedded with the soft white of silence and night.

Behind me, I could hear Yankee nosing open the gate, and my left hand withdrew from the pocket of the P-coat and dropped to my waist and onto his massive head. Through his head, I could feel the gentle uncontrolled wag of his hind end that had almost no tail to wag.

A slender hand slid down into my right coat pocket as my mother leaned into my shoulder. Quietly, she whispered, "I felt you coming."

Boxing Day, we stood in the front bedroom turned into her weaving and printing room. I was working the press when she leaned into my back. I knew from experience that she didn't want me to turn around—just be there. And listen.

She had, for some time, an uneasy feeling. Something in her was wrong. She wasn't alarmed, but she was worried, not for her, but for the rest of us. It was one hundred percent Mom.

That Christmas was when she let me know she knew she had cancer and would die of it. The doctors didn't figure it out for another year. So how could it be the best Christmas? Easy. I got to spend it with her, and she accepted who she was. I don't remember her ever mentioning church or anything religious again.

If you ever get to a little town in the Owens Valley, ask anyone in Bishop, CA, where Mt. Tom is. They might take you for a one or two block walk, but you can see the majestic mountain from anywhere in town. If there is a bit of snow on the top, I like to think it is my mother with a white dress on. Her three pounds of ashes are up there—where she wanted them.

THE NEXT GOOD Christmas came the year I was eighteen. My girlfriend, Mary, was Catholic. She also would get a smitten look on her face whenever she heard the deep rumble of a Harley motorcycle go by even if it was many blocks away. She talked her parents into letting her ride on the back of the Harley when she took me to the Midnight Mass. The only reason I agreed was that it was to be all in Latin. Her being pressed against my back, as we both shivered from the cold night, had nothing to do with it. Really.

But Latin is a hard sell. So, I changed gears and wrote another short story about seeing events differently.

Here you go, Mary. Your favorite story.

FIRST RIDE

Like a puppy snuffling into a pile of week-old laundry, her nose burrowed between the beaver fur collar and the musty worn leather of his jacket. Her green eyes were shut against the wind and cold as she huddled closer to the tawny frame bundled against the winter night. The smells of burning fireplaces and freshly snowed evergreens melded with the deep stew of the old worn leather, years of saddle soap, mink-oil, sunbaked oil, and road fumes. If she moved her nose a couple of inches higher to his neck and hair, she knew she would still breathe deep the scents that went with his motorcycle.

He had ridden motorcycles since he was twelve years old. Perching on the back of his older brothers for rides bummed to school or just to go riding in the summer. At the earliest age allowed by his parents, he had secured his very own. Through the years, he had owned one kind of bike or another, always moving up and getting larger. Now, after hard work and saving, it was a six-year-old 1965 Harley Davidson salvaged from a police auction.

Over the many months of their dating, he had, while washing or polishing the machine in her parent's driveway, patiently explained to her the many features of the motorcycle. Why it was called a "74-inch," what cubic displacement meant, and what made a "Pan-Head" different from the neighbor's Honda, other than sounding so different.

Removing the top of the motor, he had carefully cleaned all the now-exposed parts. Then guided her slim young fingers over the little moving pieces as he slowly turned the motor over by pushing the kick starter by hand. With his other hand, gentle as a baby sparrow's breath, flowing over the moving tappets, her fingers sandwiched between his, he identified each felt piece of machinery as it moved, and explaining its part in the success of the workings. She put the "Pan" on top of his head and crowned him Charlie Chaplin for the day. They wrestled and tickled all over the grass of the front yard. Then she carefully polished chrome as he quietly reassembled the engine so he could go home, across the valley.

The motor thumped gently in the night as they sat stopped at a light. Her hands pushed deeper into the pockets of his leather jacket. Reaching the bottom of the pockets, she pulled back into his stomach and hugged him, flattening her body across his back. His shoulder blades flexed and slid, recognizing the hug and its communication. The light winked green, and the Harley chuffed and barked as the tableau slid away from the intersection, sinking into the inky night of the street, a warm bubble of humanity.

The bike had always sat, cold, in the driveway of her parent's house. His tawny hair only blown about from the open window of her mother's borrowed Rambler. Them dating was fine with her parents. He had become like one of the family.

But she was forbidden to ride on the motorcycle. So they had always taken the car.

The seat had been shockingly cold when she first sat down. The throbbing of the motor was not what she had expected. It had never been so... intense. Before, when it had been only her hand resting on the gas tank, it only thumped through her arm and shoulder.

Placing her feet safely on the buddy-pegs was a job first done by him grabbing her ankles and planting her feet. The excitement tingled inside her as she exchanged "be careful" and "we will" with her parents standing in the front doorway. The unsteady wobble, as he backed out of the driveway, caused her to clamp her hands tighter in his pockets. Her nerves warred between calling off the ride she had bargained for and the fear of the unknown.

A's and B's was the price she had paid for the ticket of tonight. One month before her sixteenth birthday had come and gone without so much as a candle on a cake at dinner. All she gave up without a whimper—for this one ride. A short mile and a half each way. A lifetime away from anything she had ever done. The cold December night rasped against her one exposed cheek, an experience never felt in her sheltered world, so she turned her head straight to expose both cheeks. The lone streetlight flashed off the chrome as the trio crossed Teller Road at quarter till midnight.

The parking lot was packed with cars and people. With hushed greetings to friends, they all quietly moved toward the building. The lone motorcycle rumbled slowly across to a corner and stopped. Sliding the kickstand down, he turned the key to off. Motor and headlight burbled to silence as the night wrapped around the couple sitting on the bike.

As he moved to dismount, she squeezed him softly in restraint. "Shhh," she whispered. In understanding, he relaxed as they both snuggled into the after-roar of silence, each bump of the ride relived. Each sound cataloged and preciously wrapped up and stored away in the treasure trove of her memory, knowing the chance to savor the ride would not be given on the ride home. For now, the two sat silently as the organ in the church started the Midnight Mass for the blind.

10

PUTTING THINGS TOGETHER

In photojournalism, you have a spread of photos and words. The assignment tells you how many photos to use with how many words. The initial assignment might go like this.

"These are great, Baer. How about we do these six photos and around 1,500 words."

The size of this assignment is a large spread (running over a few pages) and usually a feature article. The only assignment better is, "Let's make this a cover story. Can you do about eight or nine photos, a cover shot or two we can crop to and build it somewhere around 2,400 to 3,500 words?"

When I worked for DÉCOR Magazine, the difference between the two was a payday of $900 and $1,200. With only maybe a couple of extra hours or six. The prestige of writing the cover article has its own compensation, especially when you and your wife stumble across a small gallery in a distant country and find your magazine cover hanging *framed* in the workshop.

Remember, I said the "initial assignment."

Reality can be deflating at times.

I've had great articles go from a 6x12 (six photos and 1,200 words) to a 2x9, and end as a 250-word sidebar with no photo—

all in the span of a week. To blame the editor is wrong. Articles can move just as fast from a sidebar to a 2x8 fill or larger in the same period—just because an advertiser backed out.

The lesson isn't the fickleness of the industry but learning how to write to the numbers.

One small assignment was given to me by the best and most wonderful editor I was ever graced to work with, Kristen Stefek-Brashares. It was early in her time at DÉCOR magazine. She had asked for a 2x5. I worked up the two images, their captions, and 487-words. I was three-weeks early of the deadline—which I was known for.

I got an email the next morning. "I need 500 words. Can you fluff?"

I added the 13-word fill and sent it back. My email was only a single word: "Fluffed."

At the convention the next year, we laughed about the word "fluff." But, from then on, I learned to write to the exact word-count she ordered. It was the most challenging skill I ever learned to master as a writer.

That is… until I saw a competition.

What I didn't see was the "submit by" date.

My friend brought it to my attention two days after. But I still loved the exercise.

The assignment was to write a short story using the image of an old wooden suspension footbridge. The story had to have a beginning, a middle, and an end. The story was to be a mystery and be about murder.

Easy Peasy.

BUT—it had to be only and exactly 200-words. Including the title.

Hope you enjoy it.

OLD WOOD

The detective leaned against the rail. The soft weathering of the wood felt the same as that night.

The murder had been exactly thirty years before. The girl was only fifteen, but the killer liked them even younger. The night had been calm, but the suspension bridge had bucked and swayed as the man beat the young girl as he raped her. His fists brutalized her face and then the back of her head as he had flipped the almost dead girl and took her from behind. The bucking and beating had never subsided. The twelve years old detective had hidden in the dark at the end of the bridge.

His sister never knew he was there. She never knew he followed her. He knew where she went, how many cigarettes she had snuck from their mother's purse, and who she shared them with. Nobody ever noticed him.

Most of all, the murderer had never known he was at the end of the bridge watching. He had seen the face. It was a face he knew, the same face walking toward him across the bridge.

The detective smiled. The gun was heavy in his hand. "Good evening, Chief."

FOR THOSE FOLLOWING CLOSELY and remembering *nothing I write is a throwaway* will recognize certain aspects of my growing up.

Growing up in the backwoods gave me an understanding of how weathered wood feels.

Understanding bullies and how they eventually turn to women gave me the visceral understanding of the brutality meted out in the rape and murder of the sister.

Having been the creepy pest of a little brother, I knew about following an older sister. Knowing what she did and what she would sneak. Also understanding the invisibility of a little brother.

Revenge? Well, that just comes with several territories. Sometimes it's physical, other times…

As I said, it's great to be a published writer.

11

MEMORIES AND OTHER LOST THOUGHTS

"You don't know what memory you have lost until you remember."

— BAER CHARLTON, AMNESIA PATIENT 1996

In 1991, I got married. I brought seventeen boxes of stuff and a waterbed to the party.

For other people, the contents of the boxes would be memories. To me, it was stuff. Most of the stuff—I needed to puzzle out. I enjoyed looking at the twelve thousand slides of animals and places from all over the world—I just wasn't sure how or why I was in some of the pictures. The articles in magazines—with my byline—were interesting but could have been written by my friend Stephen King.

There was a passport with stamps spanning the globe... which I knew were forgeries. There were two diplomas from colleges, and another piece of paper I knew was pure bull shit. The certificate was my induction into the Scholastic Honor Society of Alpha Gamma Sigma. With it was a bogus report card of 31-1/3 units of 4.0, with a personal note of congratulations from the Chancellor himself.

My GPA in high school was barely above a D+.

Then there was the DD-214 (Honorable Medical Discharge) from the Navy. Thank you, but please go destroy yourself on your own time.

Then there was the seabag full of medieval armor. And some photo albums of fighting.

I was a happy camper newlywed, and most of this shit made my head hurt just thinking about it. Almost none of it made sense.

To understand this, we must go back to 1988.

I was a territory representative for a picture frame molding manufacturer. Wisely, I had gotten the job by pointing out how many potential picture framers statistically should be in the territory. *I had taken the sanity test and flunked.*

I bought a Toyota 4x4 truck with mud and snow freeway tires. The truck body had been lifted six inches, and she had an inverted blower scoop, which helped with the summer heat. She quickly earned the nickname of Big Blue. My roommate and landlady whined she wanted a roommate—not just the month's rent. Between February eighth and December fifteenth, I drove 138,000 miles. I was on the road thirty-six weeks out of those forty-five. My territory was Northern California, northern Nevada, Oregon, Washington, Idaho, Montana, and Wyoming. I would have done Hawaii too, but there were only six picture framers in the book then—and no highway to drive there.

In early March of 1989, I drove to Carson City. On Tuesday, I saw the scattered framers around the Reno area. Wednesday, I wrapped up the few left to see and started up the Mt. Rose grade toward the north end of Lake Tahoe. The snow had been falling on the pass since five that morning. Chains or traction devices were required.

I did remember crawling up the grade at a blistering speed of ten-miles-an-hour. Even with the large mud and snow tires, and in four-wheel drive—if I hit twelve, I started to slip and slide.

About three-quarters of the way up the grade, there is a turn-out and overlook. As I cautiously approached the turn-out, I could see a small blue car half-buried in the snowbank. From my towing experience, I knew a wreck when I saw one. So I pulled into the turn-out and put on my flashers.

A young woman, with her mother and aunt, had left Lake Tahoe a few hours before, trying to beat the storm. The tires were bald, and they didn't have chains—but all three of them had blue lips. They were freezing to death. I grabbed the two moving blankets, a wool blanket, and two tiny folded space blankets made of silver ghost farts. *Amazingly, they do work.*

For some reason, I could not find the towrope or my ten feet of pull chain. I opened the engine hood of the car, only to find it packed with snow. Even if I could pull them clear, the engine would never have started—it was cold enough to make my fingertips stick to the metal.

I told them I would go as fast as I could to Incline Village and bring back a tow truck.

A few minutes later, they pulled me off the guardrail. A truck coming down the grade had hit my truck—with me on the other side. The driver admitted to driving thirty-five-miles-an-hour. He had no chains or four-wheel drive.

I spent the next year or so in surgeries and staying alive. My general practitioner doctor asked me to meet him for a few Wednesday lunches. It was the only positive thing I had to look forward to. We had lunch for many months. Whether he knew he was saving my life or not, we developed a rare and wonderful friendship.

Among many other wonderful things visited on my body, the concussion was overlooked during the first critical week, month, and year. Getting through each day and burning up twenty pounds of ice on the surgical sites was the only to-dos I focused on each day. Besides, how would I know if I didn't remember vast parts of my last two decades? The small leaks didn't become life-threatening or affect my speech or balance.

Hell, the balance was taken care of with me grabbing anything or anybody to hold onto as I walked.

Memory loss, as Hollywood portrays, is global amnesia. Mine was more bits and pieces here and there, with whole years for holes. Events or activities about my day-to-day life (Food preferences, how I wore my T-shirt, and comb my hair, or not.) had threads that ran a long way back. Small stuff like being a photojournalist, the Navy, college—not needed.

Shortly after I had gotten married, I was forwarded a letter from New Zealand. The letter was chatty, with references to things done in the past and how it was great my being there.

Me? New Zealand? *Me*?

Sure enough, there were photos. So I cautiously wrote back and explained about an accident and may have a little bit of memory loss…

Eventually, something called *Prodigy* came along, and the three-month cycle of letter to letter became overnight. I would write Lila an email and then go to bed. The next evening after work, there was a reply. As each pearl of memory threaded back onto the mental necklace, other necklaces and bracelets started as well.

For a long while, I graphed out what I knew of each year since 1970. I was comfortable with the sixties, or at least my sister was comfortable with telling me the way I should remember things. *I have since found out we have different views of ordinary events.* This explains why two people standing side by side, and looking at the same event, can have two different stories about what happened. It can be critical or just a side note in a police detective story.

Somewhere along the way, I met, on the Internet, a man in South Africa. He is a terrific graphic artist who had done the covers of a few of my books. He was thrown from a car hit by a lorry at over one-hundred-kilometers-an-hour. The seat belt probably would have killed him. He now wears a seat belt to keep his body in the wheelchair when he falls asleep at the computer.

We started a game about memories. We would choose a year and season or month. The other has a few days to remember what was going on in their life. Using Google is allowed, as sometimes, if you remember what was in the news, then you can remember what you were doing. At least, it has worked for David and me.

The year 1975 is still a huge black hole for me. I had hoped as I write my Hooker series, I would get to 1975 in San Jose and finally get a tickle. Usually, I get a panic attack, and my legs shake. It's a work in progress and part of the brain damage triggering the PTSD.

JUST WHEN YOU think you have done pretty damn well; life gives you a body check to remind you there is still much work to do.

Recently, I was asked to be a keynote speaker at my old university... yeah, the second bogus diploma. It turned out, I not only did well but had a great time doing it. So armed with enough memories of going to the University of California at Irvine, as well as a few stories about the Navy and being a writer... I accepted. The dinner was to honor the veterans who were getting their education there. And to round out the room—throw in a few dignitaries. Why not, I can get anyone to stick their little finger in their ear and wiggle it around… (I'll explain in a moment).

As the clock was ticking down, and people were flooding in, I could feel my chest start to tighten. The next step was for a baby elephant to begin pushing a brick through my chest. I was headed for a large-scale anxiety attack. Bolting out of the room before my mind started the worst-case scenario of paramedics pounding on my chest in front of seven-hundred people who came to hear me speak, not die—I went for a walk.

The long hallway to the bathroom was quiet. There was a certainty about the wide carpet and the tall concrete walls. The sound was absorbed, and I drew in the calm. The building is a block long, and the distance to the bathroom was what I needed. I little cold water on my face and behind my ears, and I felt much better. The chest was down to a dull ache.

The dinner I was addressing wasn't the only one in the building. As I walked past a long table with a few women seated there, checking people in, I stopped. My mind was totally blank. I looked over at one of the women and then turned. "Your name is Stacy," I stated.

She smiled with a smirk, and in a friendly way, patronized me. "Of course, it is, Baer."

My mind was racing. I sort memories in images, and her face wasn't fitting anything I remembered about going to college. In fact, I was confused by the image I did bring up. She was wearing a scarf all around her face.

Another image flashed through my mind. It was a painting in the Royal Portrait Gallery in England. It is of a woman in a deep green dress with a headscarf and hood. The title is something like *Lady in a Wimple*.

I stepped over to the table. "You always wore a wimple."

Now her face reflected confusion as she slightly turned her head. Looking at me out of the corner of her eye, she acknowledged the statement. I knew her from my years in the Society of

Creative Anachronism. We had dressed medieval together. I glanced at my watch and quickly explained I had been in an accident and lost my mind. But, if she talked to our mutual friend, Albra, she'd explain what happened.

As I rushed down the rest of the long hall, I started to curse... *"Memories, not mind. Memory. Stupid, stupid old Baer."* Thank gracious I had the right name... mine, not hers. She probably still thinks I had lost my mind.

For anyone else, remembering an old friend would be a small thing surrounded by pleasantries like, "So nice to see you again." I'm sure Stacy didn't give it much thought. But for me to remember a face... and then put a name to it was momentous. Especially on that night, at that moment, and in that circumstance.

My talk that night was about Little Things that are Big Things, and Big Things that Aren't. I started the speech wearing a dark sport coat over my arm braces. In a gorilla sort of way, I looked like a regular guy.

I had two friends with me as my guests. Their job was to watch the crowd, and later, I would ask them how people responded at certain times. They didn't know what was coming, so the reactions would have to be obvious for them to notice.

AUTHOR'S NOTE: At the time, I was a Toastmaster, and this was my 30-minute speech.

I started talking about how we have beliefs about the importance of things. To explain, I asked if everyone would join me and do something small—something we have all done thousands of times and never thought about it. I reached up and stuck the little finger of my left hand in my ear. As I wiggled the finger in my ear, I watched the crowd. Many of the suits were slow to respond, but when their wife had her finger in her ear—the term "Yes, dear" takes over. The entire room had a finger in their ear. Nobody was laughing, but I could tell everyone was enjoying doing something silly. I didn't need an icebreaker joke.

I pulled the finger out. "Felt good, didn't it?" There were many nods and smiles. I went on to explain about how it was such a little thing for the finger—but the ear feels so much better. It's a case of a little thing and a larger thing.

Next, I apologized. I'm the kind of guy who isn't used to suits, and I was going to overheat in the sport coat. I stepped to the edge of the stage behind the pedestal. My friend helped me take off my coat. The wireless mic went live, and everyone in the room could overhear our whispering. The coat was stuck, and I ask her not to tear it. We got it off, and I stepped back on to the stage. One, I had a body mic so I could pace the long stage. Two, the black full-length arm braces that I wore outside my long sleeve powder-blue shirt were obvious.

The report later was, "They all looked like you had just slapped them. They knew you had paid for the right to be talking to them."

I went on to speak of many things that night. I talked about big things and little things in my life. I told about how getting up early in the dorms and seeing coyotes, raccoons, mice, and falcons in and around the buildings when humans weren't there. They are little things but hold huge places in living so close to a nature preserve.

I told about how one night I had been in the park situated in the center of the campus and ended sitting on one of the boulders in the park. In the predawn gray, I noticed a California red antelope and her fawn. They had felt safe enough in the park, surrounded by manmade structures, to sleep there. I watched as they quietly got up and faded away into the morning fog. I said to myself out loud, "That was worth living to see."

Out of the corner of my eye, I saw a young Asian student. She was sitting on one of the other boulders. Her pajamas were Hello Kitty, but her hoodie was UCI. She got up and left.

The next year, for graduation, I was sitting next to a large Hispanic guy. At six-foot and two-sixty, I rarely feel small. I was the tiny guy. There were about three thousand graduating. It was a big thing getting my bachelor's degree—and yet—I felt so insignificant.

About twenty feet away and two rows down, a small Asian woman stood looking at me. She smiled and waved. I waved back. I had no idea who she was. Crowds kind of work that way.

She made her way over to me, and with her little fists on her hips, in only the way small Asian girls can pull off cutely, she told the big Latino to change seats. I seem to remember her merely saying, "Move." He looked at me with a scared look, got up, and moved. She was a little thing. He was big—they traded places. There was no discussion.

She sat down but never introduced herself. She sat quietly for a few minutes. The first speaker was droning on. I'm sure it was my friend Chancellor Dan welcoming everyone.

Her voice was like sweet lemon bars—small, sweet, but with a slight twang. "Remember last spring, sitting on the big rocks until dawn. A small deer and baby were lying on the grass…"

I nodded. I was afraid to speak. I could smell the morning's grass and ocean fog. I also remembered why I had been there in the first place.

She continued. "After the two deer left, you said seeing them was worth living for."

I nodded. It had been one of my biggest epiphanies.

"That night, I was on my way to the engineering building." She didn't have to say anymore. The building was eighty feet from the roof to the hard asphalt below. There was only one reason a student goes there at night—unless you were studying computers.

"I saw you sitting on the big rock. I wondered what you were waiting for... so I stayed." She slipped her hand into mine. "Thank you."

For years, I was ashamed of having not told her my truth. I, too, had been heading for the same building with the same purpose.

We sat there holding hands for the rest of the graduation. The large graduation was now proportioned to its respectable size.

Small things can be big, and big things only need perspective to see them in their proper scale.

In closing my speech, I invited everyone to join me one last time in the small thing. I stuck my left little finger in my ear. As one, the crowd joined me—there were no hesitations. The smiles and smirks were those of those who shared a joke or an understanding.

I told them it was just a little thing for most people. But for me—I held up my right little finger—it is also a huge thing. I brought my right hand toward my right ear. It now stops about three-agonizing-inches short.

It's those little things you never think about.

Sometimes, it is the little things you can't get out of your head. Since the night of the speech, the diminutive Asian student has been sitting on my shoulder. She kept talking about the engineering building and computers. Her presence was young but mature. Enjoy her transmogrification in *Flat Tide*.

It was this gestalt I had used in *Stoneheart*. The main character is riding with one of the Marines he served with. The young man had lost both of his legs. To drive, he was using a lever to control the gas and brake. The other hand was steering.

Stone, the main character, rolls down the window and rests

his arm in the window. The young Marine says, "I think that's what I miss most about my legs."

Stone looked over at the kid who nudged his chin at the open window. "Rolling down the window and hanging one arm out and steering with one finger with the other draped over your girl's shoulders. Just driving around on a summer night, listening to the radio down low."

Stone looked at the window and at the kid with one hand driving, and the other controlling the lever that pushed the accelerator or brake. He thought about all the injuries, and how everyone thinks about the guy with two hooks and wonders about getting dressed, but not about going to the bathroom and wiping themselves. It's the little things. Hanging your arm out of the window, or feeling the sand between your toes, it's never the big ones like seeing your child's face as they grow up, or being able even to hold a child or make love to your spouse... It is always the littlest things that affect you the most. Stone's right hand washed over the left side of his face, the side that couldn't smile, or feel, or get a date on a Saturday night. It was the small things that could make your life take a stumble.

LITTLE THINGS CAN BE big things in a storyline. Something as simple as a flat tire can create annoying tension or can be traumatic and pivotal.

On a lazy Sunday afternoon, a flat tire discovered when just running up to the store for some milk and eggs for the morning can be annoying. Add an on-going, teeth-gritting, tongue-biting quarrel about the lack of taking care of maintenance... and you have tension. Acid gut tension.

Take that flat out for a spin on the freeway, and it becomes a *flup flup flup* to the side of the road and a call for a tow service. But, add in rain and a young couple rushing because she's about to drop a kid… blow the tire and spin-dance with a few other cars. Now you have a huge pivot in a storyline.

Almost all of us have had a flat tire at one time or another. I hope all of yours have been the discovered flat in the parking lot or driveway at home. But we relate to the gut-punch—a little thing, given the circumstances, can be life-altering.

12

PUTTING IT ALL TOGETHER

In 1966, I started a job. Eventually, somewhere along the timeline, it became more of an on-again, off-again career. Luckily, it meshed with some of my other jobs over the years. In a couple of years, I will finally retire from being an "internationally-recognized award-winning Professional Picture Framer."

In the USA, I am a Certified Picture Framer. In Europe, I am recognized as a Master Frame Maker. The difference between a Master and a Journeyman is that one teaches. I have taught. I have lectured. I have spoken. I have presented on six continents, and even at sea. I have given talks in several prestigious museums.

But the best are the informal talks.

The explaining about a specific frame, or why The Birth of Venus is the most important painting of the entire Renaissance. I didn't make points with the official guide that day in the Uffizi.

But then, I paid for the guided tour to learn. It didn't take long to understand the Russian schoolgirl was hired only because she spoke broken English.

The next fun time in a museum was making up a story about a pastural scene in Lisbon. The title plaque was only in

Portuguese. By the lack of words, I could tell it said only something like "The Pasture" by Some Kindof Painter 1785. My wife had heard my runs of bullshit before and wandered off. I explained the rolling hills hiding the city from the birthplace of the squire Alfonso de Sevilla Protecio, the first squire to die in Jerusalem during the second Crusade. Or something as deep and stinky, but when told right, is so Gothically romantic.

You see, writing stories and picture framing are more similar than different. Both are about telling a story.

Writing is about telling the story. But picture framing, good picture framing, is about telling the story of the art—better.

Before I turn you loose on an example of storytelling and framing, here is one last experience.

We travel a lot. Across the world, the only buildings surviving for a thousand years are buildings of importance. These are almost exclusively castles, temples, churches, shrines, and edifices to gods. (Rome, Athens, The Great Wall, and Giza are exceptions) The pyramids in Latin and South America fall into the categories of temples and edifices.

If you take one of those bus tours in Europe, fourteen cities in nine days, I can guarantee you will see the above in profusion.

If you are lucky, you will also see cheese being aged (overly exciting), along with caverns of barrels of wine. You get what you pay for.

To all of you novices to world travel, one fair warning. No matter where you go, the Internet was there twenty years before you.

Before that, Hollywood.

So, careful what you say—the world, if not speaks, at least understands English. Enough. And you will never know who is listening.

I DRINK COFFEE AND MAKE SHIT UP

SO, HERE WE GO.

In 2006, my wife and I were on a cruise. It's not our usual style to take a bus excursion, but the port was meh, and the trip to Sevilla looked interesting. At least mildly.

The "highlight" was The Cathedral of Saint Mary of the See, better known as Seville Cathedral.

Interestingly, it was initially built by the Moors as a mosque. In its day, the Almohad Mosque was one of the Blue or Great mosques. The domed north end is all that still exists of the original interior. Outside, the original minaret, built to resemble the minaret in Marrakesh, still stands. When the Spanish reconquered southern Spain, they converted the minaret to a Christian bell tower.

As an American, this is a must-see. Buried in one of the darkest corners of the cathedral are four statues about twelve feet tall. They are holding on their shoulders a large stretcher affair. In the dim light, you will find a large, unremarkable, sarcophagus. Inside the marble sarcophagus is the coffin holding the remains of an Italian who sailed for Portugal but died in Spain. If you don't want to go but want to see what it looks like to be wanted by three countries, you can look up the tomb of Christopher Columbus. Most of the tourists don't even notice the giant sculptures.

The reason he is still held aloft is that all three countries have reason to lay claim to him. Spain is unwilling to give him up but also is unwilling to bury him.

So, there we were, a busload of tourists, waiting in the courtyard with about a half-dozen other tours. Everyone had taken the obligatory photos of the tree, the bell tower, the stones at their feet, the doors, the west wall of the cathedral, and the crowd. A few hundred people who had been doing nothing but sitting on a bus were bored standing in the fresh air.

A woman, standing a few feet away, with another tour, rolled her eyes and groaned. "Cathedral, mosque, castle, mosque, church, cathedral, castle… Don't these people have anything else to show us?"

She wasn't asking a real question. She was only venting her frustration and boredom. Her flat accent marked her as middle of the Midwest. Probably Ohio… or somewhere equally fast-paced and exciting on a Saturday morning. I couldn't leave it alone. Even as my wife stepped on my toe and pulled at my elbow, I leaned over conspiratorially.

In my worst mangling of my grandfather's East-end London accent, I explained the lack of variety to the American as she batted her double false lashes at the man who also spoke English.

"Well, love. Just a wee march away, there used to stand the home and workshop of Geppetto Antonio Badtapas Christoph de la Madrid y Matador, the world's most famous shoemaker to the kings and queens of Europe. Unfortunately, in the year 1492, after Christopher left and nobody would rent the outbuilding, the city claimed it all. They tore it all down and paved it over into a parking lot. The same parking lot the buses are all parked on today."

She only blinked—many times.

Her face, on the other hand, became a Cirque du Soleil show of contortions. The wide trapeze of awe, to the tight ball of a frown, as she fought with her decision. Had I revealed a hidden truth, or had the quirky Englishman pulled her leg?

Essentially, I had *Yankeed* her chain.

For the next hour, every time she saw me inside the cathedral, her face went through many displays of the same. I sincerely hope she eventually put together the date, the parking lot, and such a ridiculous name. But, maybe not. I would love to be a fly on the wall as she retold the story to her friends over lunch.

. . .

I DRINK COFFEE AND MAKE SHIT UP

Okay, so I lied about that being the last family story. But only to point out the expanse of small frames and old photos that ran down our hall when I was about fifteen.

They looked like they might have been family photos from the end of the previous century until about the depression. They were none. My mother had bought all the small photo frames in an antique shop, and the owner had thrown in enough old photos to fill the frames. Our "ancestors" were seafarers to cowboys in wooly chaps to even "great-uncle" Albert the Fifth. The stories ran all over the wall and down into the gutter at the whim of the teller. My father just ignored them.

So, from an early age, I learned there was a story about a picture. It may not be *THE* story, but only "a" story.

As I framed many old photos, I entertained myself with making up "a" story about the picture or items being framed.

The first story, *Flight Captain*, is about my friend's father. After I showed her the story, she gave me a copy of the actual recount by her father's tail gunner. I wasn't too far off. Her father was the first pilot to fly with a prosthetic foot. Like many after World War II, he raised his hand again when his Uncle Sam needed him in Korea. They balked at his prosthetic foot, but he convinced the commanding officer of the base by taking up a small trainer and flying some fancy maneuvers over the airstrip.

Continue on for the story...

13

THE FLIGHT CAPTAIN'S MEMORY BOX

Because of the strong side winds, the captain quietly adjusted the trim wheel that would bend the rudder in a little more, causing the big plane to fly slightly crab-like over the German countryside. These were the kinds of runs he hated. A daylight bombing run over 1944 Dresden was never a pretty sight. The broken puffy cloud cover wouldn't provide any cover for the twelve large bombers, but they would hide the Messerschmitts—German fighter planes that could ruin a guy's day.

The seat seemed to burp or jump slightly, followed by a quiet voice on the intercom radio, "starting a little earlier today."

Soon the sky around the bombers bloomed with dark clouds of explosions as the antiaircraft (Ack-Ack) shells began to explode about them. The "Ack-Ack" with it accompanying "flack" of shrapnel was the usual welcome to true enemy territory and meant the fighter airplanes would be showing up soon.

"Reception committee at two o'clock high." The flight commander confirmed from the lead B-17 bomber. "Four and Three stay in close to your leads and tighten up."

I DRINK COFFEE AND MAKE SHIT UP

The squad today was made of "enders"—Front-enders with new flight crews fresh from training, and like the captain's crew, Tailenders, and on their last mission. The second set of twenty-five long months before, the captain's uniform hat had reached and exceeded the much-admired "20 mission crush."

Usually reached by closer to fifteen sweaty nerve-wracking bombing runs from Bassingbourn, England, to Germany or France and back, and usually flown in the pitch-black of night if you were lucky.

"You headed to London tonight?" he asked his copilot and second in command.

"We thought we might. Maybe see a show and make a night of it. How— *Damn!*" as the flight deck jumped hard, "about you?" As the copilot eased in a little more fuel for the four

173

engines and keyed his microphone. "Blue Squadron, Blue Squadron, Little Betty stepping right zero-two-one, zero-two-one, keep it up." As he glanced out the window to watch the squadrons break into two bombing run squads, they banked their B-17 Flying Fortress into a slow, gentle left.

The captain yelled over the sound of the 50 caliber machine guns hammering away at the attacking fighters. "I thought I might hitch a ride with you two-up as far as Elephant and Castle. I'll catch the tube over to Vickie Station from there." The huge airship jumped and bucked higher as the cabin suddenly was shot through with bits of steel, tin, and bitter December air. Daylight was like a searchlight, at the captain's right foot, shown through a hole in the nose of the airplane that was half the size of a man. He tested his controls as the plane yawed and wiggled in response.

Keying his flight mic, "Button up, boys. It's going to be a cold ride home today." Switching back to the squad channel. "Shooter, Shooter, you have joy." Turning over the guidance to the bombardiers of each bomber lying flat in the belly of each steel beast with an eye glued to a bombsight and a hand on the set of controls.

Sitting back, this was the worst time of the flight for the flight crew... as much as five long minutes of being out of control. The bombardiers could only see what was on their charts and photos and match them to their bombsights. The gunners had plenty to do and would for another hour as they defended the airship. The engineer was fussing with whatever the engineer is always fussing with during a bombing run. And the pilot and copilot feel like the most useless people in the world.

The plane lurched in a chain of shudders as its belly-load of death slid out of the racks and into free fall on their way to destiny and a meeting of their end and others. "Bombs away" came the call releasing the pilots to grab their respective wheels and replant their feet on the rudders. Two sets of eyes scanned

I DRINK COFFEE AND MAKE SHIT UP

the cockpit looking for any shift of the dials that had occurred in the last ten seconds.

Keying the command mic, the captain called out "Little Betty Blue Squad, empty and turning, two-four-zero, repeat, two-four-zero."

Four days and seventeen hours later, the captain finally hobbled gently into his barracks room on a cane. The doctors had cut away some of the side of his right leg where the shrapnel had torn up the calf and removed the small right toe that had suffered some shrapnel and frostbite. All in all, he considered himself lucky. He was finished with the bombing, and during the twin hitches, he had only lost three planes and one gunner. Some squads had been completely wiped from the air.

He looked at the photo one of the crew chiefs had taken of the crew and plane when they were all just a bit younger and fresher looking. A few more days and her nose would look fresh and smooth again for the new crew.

His hands quietly removed the wings, propellers, Captain's bars, and ribbons from his uniform shirt and laid them in the Gentleman's Tray on the bureau. He slid the small fold of papers from his pants: identification papers, driver's license, medical air certificate, and his lucky ticket stub from a Yankee's game. Tonight was laundry night, and the shirt still smelled of the explosive cordite smoke from the antiaircraft guns mixed with days of sweat and the medicinal smell that hangs in a hospital.

His bandaged right hand reached out and touched the glass on the small photo in a gold frame of his girl back home.

Softly, his mind formed a hazy pillow of an idea about his not being able to fly anymore and settling down and getting married. Little did he know that in less than ten years, his country would ask him to fly bombers once again on the other side of the world in a cold country called Korea. Two of his crew would join him, but only one would rejoin him as a civilian stateside.

And the little girl who was years away from being born would remember her daddy and treasure his stories about his scars and missing toe, always.

14

ANOTHER THOUGHT

I've driven vehicles with two, four, six, ten, and eighteen wheels. Gears have ranged from automatic, centrifugal clutch, four and five gears on motorcycles, four and six in cars, and as many as twenty-four in trucks. I've driven tracked vehicles. I have flown planes with two wings and four. Technically the bi-wing Pitts has three wings. The upper wing spans over the fuselage, where the lower two attach on the sides. And let's not forget the single Rogallo wing of a hang glider—once.

I've sailed boats from an eight-foot sabot, twelve- and fourteen-foot catamarans, twenty-three foot 'J' class, thirty-seven Coronado, and a 5,078-ton four-mast sailing ship.

I've free-dived, SCUBA, and hard helmet dived around the world. My surfboard was a long gun.

But, of all the things I've done in my scattered life, one form of moving about held the most powerful place—motorcycles. I've owned nearly fifty. I've built a few from scratch. I've restored some and ridden many more than I've owned. How can you not take the opportunity to ride a 1937 Norton TT Manx Special on the part of the oldest Tour Trophy (road race) racecourse in the world? Even if it is the bloody assed freezing middle of January.

I got my first motorcycle when I was fourteen. I cleaned it up. Fixed the "starter" and drove the hell out of it. Much later, I sold my first article to RIDER magazine. It was about my first bike, which I called Beast.

With all the motorcycles I've owned, more than a few dozen, there have been times I have connected with people I would never have spoken to any other way. Most would have never even seen me. Most I would have never seen. But put a motorcycle in the middle, and something clicks.

I owned a Henderson inline-four. I think I had it running after about a week. I rode it down around the way for a lunch of carnitas burrito and coffee. An older woman, without asking, sat down at my patio table. Her eyes never left the motorcycle. Her father had owned one. It was green.

I saw an Ariel Square Four in the paper. I called. It was the guy's daily driver, but he was moving to New York. A friend dropped me off. I gave the guy $800 after I drove it around the block. Twenty miles later, with my teeth still rattling, I stopped six miles from home. A guy rushed in and asked if I were willing to sell it. I told him for twelve hundred dollars, it was his. He was back in twenty minutes. I never regretted it. The look in his eyes shown brighter than mine ever did.

Motorcycles are a funny thing. I grew up with advertisements on TV. "You meet the nicest people on a Honda." My second, third, and fourth bikes were Hondas. The first Honda was after some guy made me take some serious cash for the Beast. I was fifteen. I pooled money with my mother, and we bought a red and white step-through 50cc with leg fairing and a wire basket. Four months later, we traded up for a non-export Honda 120cc. The larger bike didn't fit on the side of the guy's helicopter—the 50 would after he stripped all the plastic off.

The next summer, Mom bought me out of the share, and I got a 305cc scrambler. She kept the 120cc until the local dealer made her an extremely sweet deal on a brand-new 175cc.

I DRINK COFFEE AND MAKE SHIT UP

I traded the 305cc for a 1952 Chevy truck. It had a custom sparkling brown paint job and a leaking rear seal. It ate a quart of reclaimed oil every 15-20 miles. My father got it, and I got a Yamaha 250 that seized the second day in Los Angeles. School was twenty miles away. The gears on the 10-speed rusted into high gear, and my thighs ballooned to almost burst the Levi's.

For twenty dollars, I bought a three-wheeled mail cart. The shell lasted almost a month. I found an orange easy chair in the back alley. The cushion as well as one leg were missing. I took the other legs off and ran some screws up through the flatbed frame into the frame of the chair. Now I could take a date somewhere. Except the gas cap was in their crotch. The answer was fill up before you pick them up.

The rear hubs were the same as a Ford Falcon. Off came the ten-inch tires, and on went the chrome rims and fifteen-inch tires. Now, the eighteen-horse engine could get the crazy contraption doing fifty on the flat—and it was freeway legal (minimum at the time was fifteen-horses).

It was a long slow drive from Pasadena to Santa Monica... but on a sunny day...

The next was a Triumph 600. I think it was a single piston. All I remember was the three-mile commute to work would numb my nuts and make my feet tingle for an hour after. My dates didn't like the vibration either. I would have given it away, but I bought a VW for $10 and was chopping it up because all I needed was the transaxle and engine.

The smoke from the cutting torch and grease brought the fire department. One guy gave me the name of a junkyard. But the other guy was lusting after the Triumph. We worked out a deal, and eventually, he had the bike when my new trike was up and running.

Connections. All different bikes—but connecting. I've seen heavy-duty bad-assed bikers honk and wave to the two little old ladies on pink Vespas. I've pulled over to make sure the guy on his motorcycle parked on the side of the road was okay. I've been that guy on the side of the road. I've had meals paid for when my license plate was several hundred miles out-of-state. I've bought meals for other bikers.

Connections.

...AND SOME THINGS REMAIN THE SAME

The old man's hand rested unmoved on the glass door handle. Liver spots blushed lightly along the wrinkles and cracks. The autumn sun glowed pale from the road grimed chrome of my '52 Harley, as mornings mud began to chalk on the dulled red paint. Small memories of steam rose from the travel-weary canvas pack strapped to my Harley's sissy bar. A long-forgotten special smile cracked and warmed across the well-farmed face of the old man as he pushed through the glass door into the diner. Little pops and cracks softly bid goodbye as the Harley's engine cooled in the now warming day.

His eyes never swept the room; knowledge guided them to the counter. His legs followed to the next empty seat. The tip of the old man's tongue, tattooed by years of nicotine, traced a damp course over his bottom lip. He neared where I sat hunched leather and Levi over a steaming cup of morning coffee. His timeworn teeth grabbed, gentle as a lover, at his bottom lip in hesitation. Resolved, the tongue retraced it track, wetter, as the time buffed overalls squeaked and farted into the vinyl seat next to me.

"Mighty nice machine." His words almost whispered, glowed with a certain reverence. "It reminds me of my old chief."

The caffeine-laden steam wafted through my nose and into my brain. The early morning ride through two hundred miles of America's flat frosted heartland still hummed in my ears.

Cold molasses coursed sluggish through my heart. Cold leather and frozen joints creaked in perfect harmony as the old farmer settled softly into the seat next to me.

I looked into a life-worn face as open as the harvested cornfields I'd just ridden through. His eyes danced with a light as strong as the coffee. He spoke, but his words fell on frozen ears. I heard him like the whisper of a long-forgotten lover in a dream.

I shook my head, breaking up the ice jam in my brain. I wiggled my little fingers in each ear, then pressed both palms against my ears to pump up pressure. All the while, this man sat quietly, sipping at his coffee. A small knowing smile played tag with his eyes and mine—a picture of patience and empathy.

I wiggled and jacked my jaw.

His voice flowed like fresh honey. "Well, are ya here now, or ya still frozen out somewhere near Steerman's Breaks?" His tempo was relaxed and easy from living time by the season.

"I think I'll live." I croaked and took another stab of hot coffee to make sure.

"Reminds me of a wild ride I took, one Christmas Eve, with ol' Dexter Hobson. I had an Indian Scout, but I'd busted the front axle, so Dex and I were riding two-up on his new Henderson "F" head Four. What a sweet machine that was." He stopped to spoon down some oatmeal the waitress had served. "As I said, it was Christmas, and Ol' Dex had gone and bought a ring for his girl, Mary Lynn. Well, during supper, Dex says he's gotta do it NOW or never. But Mary Lynn had gone with her family down St Louis way to her uncle's for the holidays. And so Dex says to me, full-on serious, 'and you're coming too.'" A look of mock, "OH MY GOD," slapped his face as we both sipped at our coffee.

It started to sink in. The probable temperature, bike, distance, and road conditions this man was talking about started to add up. The enormity of this realization sent a cold shiver through my body. A matching ripple rolled through his shoulders as he softly chuckled, his memories flooding back full bloom.

"My God, we were young."

"Crazy too!" I interjected.

"That's what I said." His face shattered in a chuckle as he wagged his head. "The frost was hard earnest when we got started. We strapped one Jerry can of gas to the front forks and tied another to my back. First, we rode on out to the new state toll road. That way, it would be a straight shot to St. Lou, and the frozen oil-packed gravel would be like riding on asphalt. Even riding two-up, that "F" head could really fly." [Geez, and I worry about gravel in the corners.] The *hot* coffee I sipped began to taste better with each piece of this tale.

"About midnight, the full moon came up. This was lucky for us, 'cause about an hour later, the headlight blew. By that time, there was no traffic, and we were too cold to give a hoot. We sang Christmas songs at the top of our lungs, just to keep warm.

"We made St. Lou about sun-up. About another hour to get directions and two frozen stiffs were standing in a warm parlor.

"Well, Mary Lynn, Dex's girl, came downstairs in her pink robe and fuzzy slippers. I'll never forget her. She looked like an angel. She came into the parlor with the rest of the family in tow.

"Well, son, Ol' Dex was so nervous and frozen, he couldn't bend his knee. All he could do was stand there like a big dumb ox holding out that $9 ring in its little box and listen to his teeth chatter. Everyone knew what he was there for. It seemed like hours before Mary Lynn came to his rescue. That sweet thing just blushed and softly said, 'yes'…"

Soft and gentle, he sighed with wet eyes focused on a distant time. The silence hung thick and sweet between this farmer, his memories, and me. "We got sick as dogs, but it was still the best darn Christmas I ever had."

My hand rested unmoved on the glass door handle. The Southern California sun warmed slowly off the road-soiled Connecticut license plates. Through the road grime pulsed the hot red of a Suzuki Katana. The young adventurer sat leathered at the counter. And like the wheel of a motorcycle, life comes full circle.

Like I said. Connections.

To make this complete, here is the first published story. My biggest thanks to Mark Tuttle and **RIDER** magazine. Along with a special thanks to Tash Matsuoka for talking me into coming over early for lunch and the great ride. And a sweet thanks to Merrill Pierson for all your help with what could have only been a mess of my first draft—I did get better.

THE BEST TOURING MACHINE

My grandfather once told me a good piece of advice: "If you don't want to start a fight or at least a very heated discussion, then never bring up politics, religion, or redheaded women." It's always been good political advice that I have followed religiously, and I've never been caught redheaded. The fault in Grandpa's sound advice was not that he was the first Southern Baptist minister to become mayor of his town or that he married two redheads (kind of overlapping, but that's another story). The fault was he didn't know any motorcyclist who rode seriously. Not that I'm serious when I ride or write, but I do know many riders that take their riding seriously and take their views and opinions even more seriously.

Such was the case just the other day when a letter burned its way across the pages of a tour magazine. It set off a heated discussion overloading the air-conditioner in the bike shop and drove me to the sanity of five fifteen freeway traffic in L.A. on a hot Friday afternoon. The letter had raised the question, "What was the *best* touring machine?" The parking lot had the range from a 250 Rebel to Wings, Ventures, Cavalcades, and hogs. I bailed out with half a cup of coffee left.

The electric fan hummed quietly, and the tape deck lulled softly in the stop-and-stop traffic of evacuating Los Angeles. I thought back on the many bikes of my past, some large and some small. I searched for the one that was the best touring machine. Maybe it was the 305 Dream I started college on. Or the 74 I cruised the freeways of my late teens on. The Indian Chief I pushed a lot, the VW trike I toured the states on, or the Nitro Express Thumpers.

Bikes, I have learned, are a lot like most experiences; they come at the right time and are the best for that time, and only you can decide how that is. But like most or all experiences, the first one is the best.

I first met her in a friend's garage. She was covered with dirty laundry. I guess it might have had something to do with the cute, pink-satin-and-lace number hanging from her rearview mirror, but since I was only thirteen, I doubt it. I think it had more to do with the low-slung Marlon Brando seat, the springer front end, and the ratchet-return kick start.

I guess it was a case of love at first sight. My friend couldn't understand it. He'd go watch TV, and I'd sit and watch the bike. The widespread of the longhorn style handlebars had a manly look that melted the steel of my loyalty to *Gilligan's Isle.* I yearned for the ownership of this fine piece of iron and rubber.

I ached to feel the 50cc of thundering power between my legs, the power that I knew would thrash the universe. This was what dreams were made of. This was *power.* This was what I wanted with my whole being. And this was what I could have for $10 and my pocketknife.

Over the next few weeks, I got to know my way around my prize possession. It was a Wizard. Said so on the split tanks. Year? Unknown. It was originally purchased from Western Auto—who quickly denied having any knowledge of ever seeing one, much less selling one. We guessed at the 50cc. It looked like the stand-up gasoline motor for the original Westinghouse gas-driven washing machine. The drive was most unusual, though. It was all V-belt driven. From the engine to the centrifugal clutch was one V-belt, and then another V-belt went from the three-inch pulley on the clutch to a 25-inch pulley sitting beside and attached to the rim.

The bike's saving grace was the good condition of the rubber. The bad news was the ratchet teeth had long been clashed off. The kick starter was no good, and you can't push-start a centrifugal clutch. But you can't stop a 13-year-old Brando, either.

A few Saturdays and twenty-some-odd lawns later, I got the starter ratchet wheel out of hock at the welding shop where they had attached a notched, pull-start pulley. I raced home and attached the wheel, with visions of firing up the thundering beast rolling through my head. I was, after more than a month of ownership, primed and ready for ignition.

The Beast, as it had become affectionately called, was also ready. It had received many loving and careful cleanings, polishes, and lubes. The fuel-to-oil mixture was hopefully right, and the spark plug was new and gapped to the proper double-matchbook-thickness. A four-foot piece of new cotton rope attached to a fine piece of ash, cut from the end of Dad's new shovel, and I was ready.

I set the mix, then the choke, carefully wrapped the rope on the pulley, and set my stance. Carefully, I set and reset my left hand, cross tank, on the pull handle. Gripping the throttle with my right hand and with great concentration, I placed the tip of my tongue, so it just peeked out of the corner of my mouth. My body filled with the tension and excitement of the moment. The muscles of my arms and back bunched for the effort of the moment—the moment that would mark my passage into manhood. Dawn a new decade! A new life! A more glorious... I pulled!

I missed the compression stroke. The first three and a half feet of the rope, the pull handle, and my left fist collided with my nose and left eye, leaving them bloody, black and purple, and both swollen shut for many days.

The last six inches of the pull rope caught the compression, with some painful results.

The other three and a half feet rewound faster than I'd unwound them. This left the top sides of four fingers, the side of one thumb, and three nails sheared off somewhere near the bottom of the gas tank on the way to melding the rest of the hand into the ratchet system. The unnatural twist to the body wrenched the right shoulder socket hard enough that it still bothered me when school started a whole summer later. But it also put my ear closer to the engine as the Beast snorted once, twice, then farted a couple of times and grumbled into a deathly silence.

Success was mine to be had!

I untangled my mangled ego and reached for the pull cord. The pull handle slithered out of my senseless left hand. The right replaced it immediately. I checked the proper placement of the rope and pulled with all my heart.

The Beast stirred as I grabbed and feathered the throttle, coaxing life. It roared into life with a banging that would wake the dead.

Finally, Beast settled down to a healthy rumble that set the local dogs' ears on edge and provided an audio anesthesia to match my stupid self-satisfied grin. I sat there peacefully, smiling and mentally drifting as I slowly low-revved Beast through her first warm-up in over two years. I was oblivious to the blood staining my parent's patio and to my body, which was going into shock. Success was mine, and the sounds emanating from—

Beast went proof.

Pfut-BANG!! And silence! Beast had died.

Not just an ordinary death, but one of expulsion. She had spit out her own life force! The spark plug lay resting on top of the finned head, still attached to the plug wire. I stared with my right eye at the treasonous plug in amazement, then passed out.

I eventually got the hang of safely cross tank starting Beast. I even learned to start him on the first pull more times than not. The mix I learned to gauge with the weather, and the choke had a way of working itself back on about every five miles or so. And the spark plug spitting trick was a mystery never solved. I just always packed a 13/16th Spark plug wrench in my hip pocket (the one Mom kept patching and reinforcing).

Beast and I toured many a road together. We may not have done the world in *reality*, but those 26-inch balloon tires covered every back road west of town and many roads east of town, too. It may have *looked* a lot like a Harley 45 messenger with a Westinghouse 50cc engine and a Rube Goldberg drive system, but it really was the world by the tail and a Wizard named Beast.

So, in answer to the question that starts so many arguments in so many tour shops for so many riders: For my money, the best one is always the first one, because it's the one you'll never forget.

I love you, Beast, wherever you are.

15

LUNCH, COFFEE, AND WORLD TRAVEL

Okay, you got this far, so here comes the preachy shit.
All right, those seven people just closed their books and will be taking them to Goodwill next week. So, we're safe.

First, yes, this is the chapter about world travel. So, for all of you who keep saying, "I've always wanted to go to _____," here is my lesson. But first, we need to get through a little shopping, lunch, and shopping. But trust me, it will all make sense.

For all of you who are starting to place a protest about this being a book about writing… you need to go back to the beginning and start over. Obviously, you haven't been paying attention. And for you, this is the chapter about the journey with no signposts.

First, the test.

This is the test I always ask of people who tell me they always wanted to go somewhere in the world.

The number one place is Paris… until they find out the people there speak French. Then it might change to London. Go figure.

But my questions go like this:

1. What is your favorite restaurant?
2. Who is your favorite waiter or waitress there?
3. Do you have a current passport? (You would be surprised how many people want to go to Paris, but don't have a passport.)
4. Where do you buy gas?
5. What is your usual food market? Extra points for naming three checkers. Bonus points for naming one of the butchers or produce person.
6. Which European countries want you to get a Visa before you leave the USA?
7. Who is your favorite gas station attendant?
8. What is your mail person's name? Bonus points if you know a post office counterperson's name.
9. Which person, on USA money, spent more time in Paris than as the President of the United States?
10. What is your favorite restaurant food?

I'll explain the answers later.

THE SUMMER my sister was twenty, I was sixteen. She worked at one of the few steakhouses in town. I don't know if I worked as much as I enjoyed being one of the two busboys. Our job was to make sure everybody's water glass was three-quarters full. If they were having coffee after dinner, make sure they were at least offered a second cup. And, of course, bus and reset the tables in under ten minutes. I had an in. My sister was the most popular waitress. Not the busiest. That would have been the older gal, Roberta. Between the two, the third only got a few tables.

Roberta was a great waitress. But my sister was known, or I should say, most people in town knew our family. I smiled. She talked. I got one-tenth of her tips. Or the two busboys got a cut of the waitress's tips. The third waitress coughed up a few bucks. We felt bad for her. Us busboys were making more than her.

A steak and lobster dinner with a loaded baked potato cost about ten bucks. Coffee included. There were some Saturday night regulars. Bennie owned the lumberyard. His party was always two or four. He always slipped my sister at least a twenty, and me a ten. And that was before he hit the table with a fifty or hundred. The first hundred I ever saw was from Bennie. When school started, he knew I'd drop down to my usual two after school jobs—so he slipped me a full crisp Benjamin. I don't think I spent it until after the New Year.

Then there was the tip from Kurt for horrible, embarrassing service. They were new to town. I liked hanging out with his stepdaughter. She was new in town and just as shy as I was. I walked her to the movie one night. Without thinking about it, we held hands while I walked her the five blocks to her home. Her folks owned a motel, and they lived behind the office. I liked her mom and Kurt. He had a jovial way of teasing and groaned in appreciation at my puns.

Monday at school, the rumor mill had started. By the third period, we had had sex. The fourth had her pregnant. By the sixth period, she had found me and slapped my face, thinking I had been spreading the rumor. By the next week, a couple of other girls had set her straight about both the rumor and my innocence. We were friends again… but no more dating.

Kim's stepfather, Kurt, had reserved a large table for a family gathering. I think Kim was babysitting her little brother and the motel. It was all adults. Kurt introduced me around. Brothers, sisters, uncle or aunt, and his mother. She was the party's honoree. It was her birthday. Maybe in her seventies or more. She was a regal and gracious woman. Her dress was backless black lace. Not what we usually saw in the Mule Capital of the World.

Dinner finished, and I was getting around to the coffees. I

had moved in with a full cup of hot coffee. She turned to tell me she changed her mind and would like a cup, not knowing I was so close.

She got the entire cup of hot coffee down her back.

I froze in horror. She stood in a shot. I'm sure the hot coffee went straight down to drench her panties. She reached before I could move and gripped my arm. She pulled me in and whispered hoarsely enough for everyone to hear. "I haven't had a hot date in years. But I would rather have my coffee in a cup, please."

My sister was there in a heartbeat with a few large fluffy napkins. After the shock, and a trip to the lady's room, the party was back at full steam. I really liked the family.

As they were leaving, Kurt pressed a twenty into my hand. "I know you didn't mean to, but I haven't seen her move like that since I was a kid." He winked and went to get their car.

She was the last. She wrapped her arms around mine and asked for me to walk her out. She thanked me for the most memorable dinner since her husband proposed. I blushed, and she slipped something in my pocket. And then, at the car, she rose on her toes as she pulled me down. She kissed me on the cheek and then kissed my collar. She had put on fresh red lipstick. She was a class act.

I found her fifty in my pocket when I got home. I asked Kim to meet me for lunch a week later. I spent the fifty and told her how much I liked her grandmother.

The next year, I graduated from high school and was working the graveyard shift at Welch's Pancake House. The other end of town and the spectrum.

This is where I started falling in love with crusty older waitresses who had been doing the job longer than I'd been alive.

As a dishwasher, busboy, and sometimes getting to learn cooking, I saw it all.

At one-ten in the morning, a few days in the week, you could hear the big rig park across the street. The diced ham, Ortega chilies, and six eggs whipped with a tablespoon of cayenne pepper spread out on the grill. Let it cackle while four slices of wheat toast dropped into the toaster. No potatoes, but a bowl of canned peaches. When the eggs were ready, five slices of American cheese were laid on the omelet and folded over.

The waitress with red hair and white roots, poured a coffee and picked up the platter of food. Turning, she laid it down at the end of the counter as the man sat.

His comment was always the same. "The coffee's cold."

One night, she had Joe the cook stick the heavy ceramic coffee mug in the broiler. She delivered the mug to the Formica counter almost red-hot. The coffee started to boil as she poured it in. The food hit the counter seconds later as the man slid into the seat.

He grabbed the mug and then pulled up a couple of napkins. He dipped the napkins in the ice water he never drank and wrapped the mug handle. He sipped at the coffee and set the mug back down on the brown ring burned into the indestructible Formica. "Perfect." The blisters on his lips were only scabs when he came in next.

The following week, she poured and served the omelet an hour before he arrived. He never said anything but "Perfect."

The owner told me over Christmas that they had gotten married. I guess the twelve years of serving, bitching, burning, and chilling had been the courtship.

AT NINETEEN, I moved into the famous house in East Los Angeles. What I didn't write about were the twenty-six dead bushes in the backyard. I whacked them down to about two feet high with the intent of digging them out later. I watered the lawn, and suddenly, I had long-stem American Beauty roses in seven colors.

Five to eight meals a week, I ate at Bob's Big Boy. The morning I discovered the roses, I was headed for breakfast. I grabbed a box, cut roses, and filled the box. Probably about four dozen.

The waitresses were young enough to be pleasing on the eyes, but only a few were old enough to be moved by the flowers. I didn't mean for it to happen, but we came to an unspoken game. In those days, tips were usually about a dime. Rarely a quarter.

If the roses kept coming, they wouldn't let me tip. So I hid the tip. And the game started.

If I could pay my bill, walk—not run, and make it to my motorcycle, then they had to accept the tip I hid. If they could run and catch me, I had to take it back. It was a fun game and a special relationship with several gals. Some married, but most not. But all of them a family of sorts.

In the eighties, with hundreds of small cafés and restaurants under my belt, I started writing about them. They were the Mom & Pops, the greasy spoons, holes in the walls, and cozy cafés of my wanderings.

I found I gravitated toward those with at least a small counter. The kind where a few old farts gathered every morning and milked their cup of coffee while they bitched, moaned, and solved the problems of the world. A weathered waitress looked at me with a worn smile and said it best. "Cookie started this joint after he got back from the South Pacific." (She meant WWII). These bozos had jobs back then, but their butts were drawn like magnets to those chairs. They probably didn't talk to one another in high school, but you can't shut them up now. They're all prickly and argue like the idiots up in Washington DC, only here they have hard shells and the bullets and barbs just wander off and die. I call them my Crabby Congressmen.

Most of the best places I found had their version of a Congress of Counter Crustaceans. Interestingly, they had logically hashed out certain problems, and it would behoove some real elected officials to go sit in and listen to some answers.

As a side note about counters and the people they attract. Shortly after the turn of this century, Denny's thought they would discourage the hours-long nesting of the congresses and remodel for the twenty-first century. They started ripping out the counters. Not far into the experiment, they discovered how wrong they were. The compromise became shorter counters and more booths. Then some idiot had a brain fart and figured if they raised the counter to bar height, the wait staff saw eye-to-eye with the customers, and they could hide more storage under the counters.

Now, most of the waitresses can't see if your coffee mug is full. So, either the customer is shorted, or the waitress must pick up the mug and bring it behind the counter to fill it. This is where a spill ruins a large stack of napkins or placemats, contaminates a tray of silverware, or spectacularly destroys their new lifeline—the computer printer for ordering take-out on-line. The resulting sparks and explosion made the morning's second cup of coffee redundant.

THERE WAS a café in Northern California. It stood on a road defining the southern edge of Santa Rosa. It was a hopping place with maybe six or eight customers when I tripped over it. The sign on top of the building was dark, but it did say CAFÉ. I would have driven past, except for the cars nosed up in the parking lot, and the lights inside were on, even at just after six in the morning.

As I started to sit at the counter, one of the other customers, with two napkins tucked in his collar to protect his suit, turned.

He pointed. "The coffee is over there, and that's May. Tell her what you would like, and if she can make it, she will or tell you no." He returned to his own food and newspaper.

When in the area, it became the only place to eat breakfast.

There was a five-gallon glass water bottle, sitting on a small table by the door, with the top cut off. It was more than half-full of money—bills floating on a solid bed of coins. Order what you want. May would cook what she could. Figure out what it was worth to you and make your own change—May was busy cooking.

She got the eggs from her sister-in-law and their egg farm. No money. Just helping keep the sister busy.

The pork came from her uncle's family pig farm and meat market. No money. Just helping keep May having fun.

The bread guy had served with her husband in North Africa, Italy, and France on their way to Berlin. Evidently, they had served in 4-H, Boy Scouts, hunting anything, and school since the first grade together. No money. It was family.

The café sat out on the road fronting the twenty or so acres of homestead. It hadn't been open since her husband was alive. She had a peaceful life of widowed solitude a hundred yards back through the trees.

One morning she was making coffee when the coffeemaker conked out. The stove was down to only one burner, and the oven was flakey even when her husband was alive. But she knew everything worked up at the café.

In the early morning gray, she carried her can of coffee and a bag of fixings up to the café. Turning on the lights, she made coffee while the griddle came up to temperature.

The bell over the door tinkled. She turned and blinked at the young man looking for the open sign. She chuckled. "Coffee's almost ready."

The young man looked at the thin film of dust on the stool. She handed him a rag. He wiped it down and continued with the empty counter. She laughed as she told me. He wiped down every stool and the entire counter. He only stopped when she put down a mug of coffee.

He sat. "Do you have a menu?"

She gave him her best auntly hard stare. "No. They taste like the crap they wrap toilet paper with. I have eggs, American cheese, bacon, and wheat toast."

He blinked in confusion. "No white toast?"

She pointed her arm. "Sure, honey. But it's two miles down the road that way. You go get it, and I'll toast it."

He blinked. He blinked again. "Wheat's fine."

Smart boy. She turned to make them breakfast.

Before the plates were on the counter, two more men were sitting at the counter. The sun was just turning the tips of the pines pink. May thought about the three eggs left and a handful of bacon.

She remembered the phone. Years before, it was connected to the house. She picked up the receiver. There was a dial tone. She made two phone calls. Help was on the way. Her second cousin would pick up bread while they brought bacon and ham.

Her sister-in-law would pick up a bale of napkins at the Pick-N-Save. She turned on the large refrigerator just in case.

The young man stood. His smile radiated his happy tummy. "How much?" The money was in his hand.

May had never taken money to cook someone a meal. She spotted the empty bus tray. Putting it up on the end of the counter, he told him whatever he thought it was worth. He peeled a few bucks and laid them in the large tub.

He muttered about it being a hell of a way to run a restaurant. She laughed. The café isn't open for business—she had only come in to cook her own breakfast. She pointed at the plate with only a few bites snuck between helping the guys at the counter.

He blushed and asked if she would be cooking the next day.

"Probably. The stove in the house is busted."

He shoveled in a few more dollars.

She smiled. "I might even have white toast. Who knows?"

When I stumbled in, she had been cooking breakfast for three years.

When the IRS or the county sent someone around to collect taxes, she pointed at the jar. When people asked about change—she pointed at the jar.

One day, a desperate scrawny kid decided it was easy money. He grabbed the whole jar, lifted, and turned to run out the door.

Everyone heard the crack.

The jar thudded back onto the table, and he grabbed at the small of his back as he stumbled out the door. A few gallons of change in a large glass jar can do some serious damage to some skinny bones and scrawny muscles.

May laughed. "He could have just cleaned out all the bills, and nobody would have moved. Some peoples jus' don't get it. This here café still ain't open for business. I'm just cooking breakfast for me and friends."

I KNOW this is running long, but I'm getting there.

When I first moved to South Pasadena, I drove the Menstrual Cycle. (The three-wheeler that used to be a little mail truck.) Every twenty-eight days, she blew a head gasket. The Chevron station was two blocks away. I would push the three-wheeler down there. They let me run it up on the hoist and swap out the gasket. Sometimes I just went down to wash the work bays, shoot the shit, or get some gas.

One day, I had a spasm in my neck. As the day progressed, it got worse. When I stopped in for gas, I was pulling my head to my left shoulder to keep the pain from dropping me to my knees.

Ken, the owner, asked me what was with my head. I told him but eased up on the neck just enough for the pain to hit. The next thing I knew, he was holding my head in the backseat of his car. I don't remember who was driving. I don't remember getting to Huntington Memorial Hospital. In the early morning, the neck was fine. The hospital kicked me out when Ken showed up to drive me home. Days later, I thought about not paying. I didn't have insurance, and nobody asked—definitely different times.

Years later, I stopped in at the Chevron. Ken's boy owned it by then. He remembered me. He remembered the night. Ken told the hospital I worked for him and put it on workman's comp.

AT ABOUT THE SAME TIME, money was tight for my roommate and me. There was a large fifty-pound bag of dog kibble in the broom closet when we moved in. Six three-inch Bisquick pancakes or oatmeal were our usual breakfast. Dinners were iffy at best.

One night I was in the grocery store a block away. The can of French onion soup, a bag of barley, and a handful of mushrooms on sale cost about forty cents. I added the soup, a bunch of water, and a handful of barley to a few cups of the kibble. Then I sliced the mushrooms over the top and added the last two slices of American cheese. I baked it for about forty-five minutes.

Tom couldn't believe I had cooked real food and dug in. I watched for the first five forkfuls before I had to try it myself. I didn't tell him what it was until I was washing the bread-loaf pan out the next night. He wound up and hit me in the arm once. Thank goodness ice was free. His hand needed it.

We never told another soul what the secret recipe was. But it did get us laid. Times were tough for the girls too.

After the fifty pounds ran out, we were doing a little better. So we only bought a twenty-pound bag. Tom moved in with his girl, and I was tired of listening to the giant rats in the attic play bowling balls all night. I moved into the house in East L.A. a month later. I left at least fifteen pounds of kibble, and the recipe taped inside the broom closet door.

IN THE EARLY EIGHTIES, I lived in the corner of a cul-de-sac in Hollywood. Four doors down lived a gal who taught first grade. I forget how we started talking, but we were. She was a step above a Plain Jane but had never been out on a date. She also had no interest. Thai food came up. She had never heard of it. At the time, most hadn't. I told her how the owners (two sisters) at the Bangkok Hut had been teaching me all about Thai food and the proper way to eat it. Chopsticks are a nasty word.

We finally agreed to go to dinner so I could introduce her to Thai food. It wasn't a date. Simply good food. Nothing more.

After work, I got home and jumped in the shower. After, as I was sitting and cooling off, I transitioned from feeling fine to I-think-I'm-going-to-die in less than fifteen minutes. The front door was open, and I was in my bathrobe face down on the floor when she showed up to go.

She told me if this was a stupid ploy to try something funny, she was going to kick me in the "man parts." I almost had the energy to chuckle at the childish genital name. She gave me two choices: ambulance or I get dressed, and she'd take me to St. Joseph's. I got my pants on. She helped with a T-shirt, and we gave up on the shoes. She was simply happy to get me into the car.

As I lay in the ER, I started realizing what she was wearing. Red shoes, red tights, red wraparound dance skirt, and red leotard. She looked like one of the girls in the dancer's dorm at college. Except they would never have worn all fire engine red.

The doctor was a slight man. His accent was full-blown Bangladesh. He was wearing a faded madras shirt, faddishly faded Levi's with a skinny beaded belt saying Lake Tahoe. The shoes were Docksider slip-on deck shoes. He asked what I had been taking. It wasn't the first time I'd had a medical person look at my beard and assume I was on some drug or another.

I weakly grabbed the neck of his plaid shirt and pulled him to me. I told him exactly what and how much I had eaten during the day, and which vitamins and doses I had taken. At two-sixty and still with a bodybuilder's body—I got my point across. Months later, he admitted I had scared the crap out of him.

He called for a blood draw.

Minutes later, he rushed back in with a plastic shot glass of potassium drink. He explained about the mineral. "Mister Charlton, you potassium too low, if you decided to sleep until morning, you would have no morning." He looked up at Linda, sitting quietly in concern. "Young lady, what you do? You suck all the potassium out of Mister Charlton?"

She became solid red from her black hair to the floor. He realized he had miss stepped and turned to see about checking me into the hospital for a few days.

Two nights later, there was a soft knock on my hospital door. Linda stood there with two shopping bags of food. The smells of curry, fried squid, shrimp, and other delights hit me hard. I raised the bed to full sitting up.

Several nurses pushed her into the room. In minutes, the room was full of nurses on the bed with Linda, in the chairs, standing, leaning, and all were eating. The Bangkok Hut was only two miles away and a vastly popular place with the hospital staff.

The room turned meekly silent when a familiar voice floated down the hall. "There better be stuffed squid left for me."

I laughed and called out. "Hurry up, TK. They're going for the last piece." Hardly true, there were six orders or more. The ladies at the Hut knew what I liked.

Linda had gone to the restaurant the night after our aborted not-a-date to explain what had happened. They sat her down and started her education. She was in love with the first bite. She was smart enough never to ask what she was being fed until after she liked it.

They told her to come back the next night and pick up a picnic bag to bring to me. They knew the smell would infiltrate all five floors, and we wouldn't be eating alone. TK Desai was one of their first customers and had corrupted the entire hospital.

As a wise person once told me, "It's not who you know that is important, but who knows you."

I would add to Mom's words: "...and knows you well enough to know what you like or need."

After being hit by a truck, I spent my next year in and out of the hospital and recovering from one surgery after another. The surgeries never stopped, only slowed down for a time.

One surgery on my back left me with only one lung. I went from being able to curl eighty-pound barbells to struggling with the creamer cup for my coffee. I swear the little motherfucker who designed those individual creamers was a twenty-something who hated older people. I've since met people with arthritis and hand problems who just stab the fuckers with a fork or knife.

There was a small breakfast place in Los Gatos. Named the Egg and I, and then the Broken Yoke or some other eggy thing. But they served omelets. I'm not saying I was a regular there, but I knew their names (even the cooks), and they knew mine.

I always quietly sat and read while I ate. After the accident, they let me work on opening the creamers, and then one of the waitresses would come along and open five or six. It was never patronizing—just helping.

So, one Saturday or Sunday with a packed house, and with my orders to stay roosting at the second seat on the counter, I worked on opening a creamer. Nobody in the place knew me. No customer could have given a rat's ass about me. Only the workers understood what I was doing. Why I was not moving but sweating like a fat boy in a steam room. Sweating so much, I had to keep drying my hands. I was focused. No sound. No peripheral vision. Only the creamer cup, my thumbnail, and a bent finger existed.

I hadn't noticed when Joanne quietly set down the plates and stood watching. I couldn't hear when the other gals noticed Joanne, knew what I was working on, and froze in place. The cooks, Frank and Charlie, let food burn while they clustered in the small window. All 140-customers stopped talking or eating. They didn't know why, but they sensed it was important.

The lid slowly peeled back.

I looked up as proud as any kid who tied his shoelaces for the first time. I smiled at Joanne—glowing. She started a slow clap. Then I realized the whole restaurant was also clapping. I turned bright red.

I'm sure most never knew what they had clapped for. But it didn't matter. They *were* *there* when something huge had happened.

YEARS LATER, my wife and I stopped to visit my old roommate and her husband. I'd once woken Cindy up, at one in the morning, to take her to a restaurant in San Jose called Just Breakfast. They were open 24/7. They served only breakfast. She knew I liked breakfast. She told me over and over for years, "If there's a restaurant out there that only serves breakfast—you'd find it."

She told my wife she was taking us to a great restaurant I had never been to. It had only opened a few months before, and I had been gone for a few years. We were good to go.

We walked in and sat down. The waitress didn't say a word

but rubbed my shoulder as she asked who wanted coffee or tea. She brought back the coffees and asked the women what they wanted to eat. She took their orders and put her book away. Cindy pointed at me, saying she had forgotten to take my order.

Joanne laughed. "Frank is already cooking his omelet."

I ignored Cindy's open mouth. I stood. "Is Charlie back there too?"

It had been about six years, but it was old home week. It's who remembers you—even when they go and finally open their own restaurant.

Okay, back to the questions.

1. What is your favorite restaurant? If you don't have a favorite, I'm guessing you always eat at home. If you don't but only eat out when you must, it's the same. Going to restaurants and getting to know the staff is the stuff of travel. If you go to Paris and only read the menu, you will only eat what you recognize from home. So, don't go.
2. Who is your favorite waiter or waitress there? See number one.
3. Do you have a current passport? Nobody is serious about wanting to travel unless they have at least gotten a passport. Just a tip here. It's better to travel domestically with a passport than just a driver's license. It identifies you as a traveler.
4. Where do you buy gas? If your answer is "wherever it's cheap," then stay home. Don't travel. There is no cheaper gas in the world than here. The $1.23/liter means about $1.65 a quart. Or seven dollars a gallon, and your rental car will always be a gas-guzzler.

Filling up a small car on the Autostrada will cost you close to eighty Euros or a hundred bucks. Stay home. But if you like to drive and like espresso coffee… you're going to love the Autostrada.

5. What is your usual food market? Extra points for naming three checkers. Bonus points for naming one of the butchers or produce person. Even the large general markets in the world are like small neighborhood stores here in the USA. Talking to the staff is always a bonus.

6. Which European countries want you to get a Visa before you leave the USA? Trick question. Your American Express and MasterCard are useless in the rest of the world. Only Visa is universal. (Author's Note: When I wrote this section in 2019, the American Passport was all you needed to travel in the EU. As of this editing, almost all of the world is shut down to Americans, and the EU is considering reinstating the need to acquire Visas to Americans. The lesson here is: Don't piss on or off your allies— even if they need your tourist dollars.)

7. Who is your favorite gas station attendant? With self-serve becoming the norm, this is less and less a criterion about talking to the people who take your money. But it helps if you do.

8. What is your mail person's name? Bonus points if you know a post office counterperson's name. The same can hold true about knowing your bank manager and cashiers as well as having them on speed dial in your phone. Bonus if you know them well enough to have their cell phone numbers too.

9. Which person, on USA money, spent more time in Paris than as the President of the United States? If you said Jefferson, you were close but not right. He

was the ambassador to France for only five years. But he served two terms (eight years) as president. He replaced the correct answer as ambassador, Benjamin Franklin. Bennie served as interim president for a day until George was sworn in as the first real president.
10. What is your favorite restaurant food? Sorry, but pizza, goulash, burritos, and snails are American foods.

You may be wondering what all this about restaurants has to do with travel or writing. It doesn't, and yet, it does.

The smaller the restaurants—the more it does. Big chains—not so much. Denny's, Big Boy, Waffle House, IHOP, and certainly not Cracker Barrel. Actually—especially not Cracker Barrel.

What smaller cafés, Mom & Pop's, holes in the walls, and other small eateries have in common is they rely almost exclusively on repeat and regular customers. The same for small neighborhood groceries, neighborhood gas stations, bars seating thirty or less, and even the flower shops. They all rely on the people whose names they remember. It's connections. Human connections.

Those who buy the cheapest gas, follow the cheapest food prices and only eat out when they must—those are the people who have few friends outside of their church or organizations they belong to. And even then, they won't know if they have any true friends until the shit hits the fan and they are left standing alone. (I covered this in the chapter about death.)

These are the people who, if they do travel abroad, only survive in large organized groups such as tours and wonder why it's always castles, cathedrals, mosques, and museums. The seventeen cities in twelve days for less than $100 a day? Go for it. It will really make you appreciate the Motel 6 afterward. You will see the sights—from your bus. You will tour castles—if you can walk fast enough. You will kiss the blarney stone—I've watched this one. The guy wasn't exactly gentle when he had to process a tourist every 78-seconds. And trust me—if you weigh more than the guy helping you—it's on you. The drop down the side of the castle is eighty-five-feet to the boulders below.

You can hear stories all the time about how this person got abused in Paris. Or that person was never treated so rudely as by the French. I've heard stories about Paris, London, Moscow, Madrid, Lisbon, and even Rome... wait, no, especially Rome. Even I will never go there again. But when you hear those stories, ask yourself about the person telling the story. How do they treat people in their neighborhood restaurant, gas station, market, or park?

I took my wife to Europe. She tends to make me be the mouth until I talk longer than forty seconds. But it was 2003 when the president drew a stupid line in the sand and said if they weren't with us, they were against us. That summer, 14,000 people died from the scorching heat in France. America had turned its back on the world. My wife just knew they hated us, and she was prepared.

We were on the Pont au Double (a bridge with a wonderful view of Notre Dame). It was a beautiful fall day. Two Asian women approached us. Their accents were Parisian. They asked if we were Americans. My wife started to say Canadian. I stopped her and replied, "Oui, American." Then they surprised us.

They took our hands. "We know you are not your president. Thank you for coming. Merci, merci, merci beaucoup." Then they asked to get their photos with us. It was the first amazing event of the day.

After, we floated our way back to the small quiche shop we had snacked in the afternoon before. The espresso was good, but the tiny shot for five Euros was a little steep. But the exceptional quiche made it all worthwhile.

The same young man was working. He remembered us. As we sat, he placed a large white mug of regular coffee in front of me, and a large mocha latte in front of my wife. He pointed at us and named the quiches we had eaten the day before. Bon. Oui.

I asked about the large off-menu mug of coffee. He reached behind the counter and held up a Starbuck's vente. The first Starbuck's in Europe had opened at eight in the morning to a line seven blocks long. There were nine barista stations. Europe and the world would never be the same again. When he served the quiche, he went and brought back his vente and pulled up a chair.

"Tell me. What did you see today?" In a single day, we had become old friends. If he told us his name, my wife probably wrote it in her journal. I do remember his family was from Turkey. But whether it was legal or not... I don't remember. But I will never forget how to get to the quiche shop. It is just a few short blocks from the magical Pont au Double.

We all have the same lives. We are born, and then we work hard at dying. How we spend the time between the two ends decides what kind of life we have. Or, if we are writers, how we write about the messy stuff in the middle or the end. Small cafés are where much of the messy "stuff" goes on.

I'm often accused of having my characters spend time in my books eating and drinking coffee. I stand guilty as charged—because much of life happens around dining tables, counters, and people talking over food or drink.

In 1986, I knew nobody on Boxing Day on the Isle of Mann but went home with three gifts from St. John's Pub. I watched a christening in an Irish pub outside Sydney, Australia. I've attended wakes in bars and pubs. I've attended weddings and proposals in coffee shops. But I've never attended anything that would cause a mother to cry at a Cracker Barrel—but I have seen grown men want to when they see the bill.

So HERE IS another tough story about life and another small café.

DIGGER'S BRAT

The small gray slivers of wood lay scattered over the threshold like so many fallen soldiers about a battlefield of time. The sun baking them to dried rot—or a memory gone white with senility. Like any threshold of importance, it foreshadowed what is inside, setting our mood to match the interior, molding our expectations, and releasing us from the constraints of the world without. Prejudice we would be, without the founding stamped on our eyes, by the entry. Tainting our vision to see only the reality supported by the universe inside. The obscuring windows dully reflecting the hard contrasts of the street below, like two old lovers slowly touching in the night. Their memories of youthful discovery, complexities washed away by the simplicity of time gone senile, yet tender in their mercy, offering comforts of hearth and soul.

As the sun battered pine door swings wide, the long screen door spring, a squeaking nag of passing decades, moaned a song of entry. The sun flashes black off the spit polish of the military shoe, passing in unseen review over the fallen of the entry. Ceremonially slow, with military cadence, the khaki slacks with creased centerlines pointing the way into the dim shaded interior of a faded memory, strode forward.

The doors RAP! *Tat-tat-pat-a-pat-pat* lends voice to the blinking eyes of the old men in white rolled sleeves and collarless mattress ticking shirts. They roost constrained in their patterned lives. The aged leather of their suspenders wears thin the material of their being. And yet, preserves the underpinnings of the honor and dignity they traded among themselves like baseball cards and lies. Softly they cling to the common camaraderie which restrains them from the final rest they fear less than the shame of being the old fools they are—for not admitting the fools they were.

The roar of the silence was broken only by the waft of greased air pushed by the slow-turning fans. Life rafts clung to by bored flies—long ago tired of the bigger game hunkered in sweat and age below. Occasionally furrowing out a landing in the ageless grease, to ride into eternity, or until some unexpected health inspector occasions to look up. A slow-moving tale of past lunches fried endlessly. Sarsaparilla's and Cony Islands anguished over by barefooted boys whose bib overalls hold secrets of rocks and toads. All long past. But they are remembered by the perfume of pickled eggs and strong pine-scented cleaner in the late afternoon. The young perfume boys never notice, but always remember as their hair thins, shoes become slippers, and they shuffle to gather in small dens of remembered sanctuary—such as The Green Grill. Still a half hour before closing, but hours before the widower, Brice Green, would shut his door for the night. Solitude is a bittersweet drink, best shared from a bottle passed around a group of old friends.

"Grill's off."

The soldiers left hand, filled with his wool hat, rested lightly, tenderly, on the chipped and faded-green Formica counter trimmed in nickel. It slid softly and remembered. The khaki trousers with knife-edged creases, small dirt smudge here and there, eased down into a memory on the stool. The boy's feet poised ready to spin the sitter and seat 360—the adult refrained. The right hand slid smooth, palm down along the time-beaten Formica pausing at the initials DB+BG—carved there long ago. Fingertips and hushed lips, tracing, and retracing the forgotten and remembered. The afternoons after school. The summers—hanging out because Bonnie had to work for her father. Never dating. The anger. The injustice of being from the wrong side of town. Or, the wrong father.

The left hand pulled gently at the well-trained riot of black curls, memories of one stolen night out behind the Grill… Confidences shared. Truths revealed… Hearts laid bare.

"I said, the grill's off for the night." Brice stood like a monument to years of greasy food and age. The hair thinned to transparent, now combed across the field instead of its original back-thrown Irish red turf. The bags and crow's-feet tallowed and shined from jaundiced candle wax, layered and built-up of time. "Can I get jya anything chilled?" His hands stuttering at wiping the large malt glass. His watery eyes reflecting the white-light box of the screen door. A set of two illuminating floodlights exposing a life lived in servitude—yet lord of the manor. The soldier recognized the guard dog at attention yet ready to cower to the chain and leash, foisted or voluntary. Probably unwanted, and yet comforting.

"How about," the dry soft voice paused as the eyes of the two men locked, "a St. Patty's iced tea, with a steak for the heart?"

The words hung fresh in the thick moldy air. Brice's eyes narrowed as the pupils widened. Slowly the malt glass flowed to the counter, sliding shuffleboard style by the weathered hand, as the two faces drew near. Ages. Years. Gray hair, all blew away in the winds of recognition. Memories of decades gone by, recognition of the uniform of today, old wars, half-forgotten angers, prejudices held, all warred with the excitement of seeing an old familiar face. Emotions, like the spirit of the body, get tired with age.

The creases about the mouth softened. Tallow flowed as on Sunday at Mass. The hazel pools shattered and deepened, the world let in. A small drop of the pool, nestled at the corner of one eye, then traced its lonesome way to the gray stubbled chino cheek.

The heat-tempered hands shyly reached forward and took hold of the younger set.

"You're the Digger's Bra…"

The soldier reflected on his father, the only French-Creole and Spanish Basque in town. His occupation had always been the county's gravedigger. And cesspool digger. Or trench digger. Or just about anything you wanted to bury, Claude Boudreaux was your man. The common saying was if it's buried in Tyler County—Digger put it there.

Funny. Over fifty-years of service, and none had bothered to ask or use his real name. Even his wife of fifty-three years called him Digger. And, when the upstart juvenile delinquent son came along—he was tagged with the name…

Digger's Brat.

It hadn't helped that his real initials were DB. "That's right, Mr. Green. It's been a long time—about twenty-six years, sir."

The tension between the two was broken, as the old lowering hands turned the young palms up. Reflections of the soft pink hands mirrored on the tiny silver Chaplin crosses pinned to the soldier's collars. The fresh rash of blisters, along the heels of the hands, in the thumb web and on the tips of the fingers, seemed out of place—a bastard child at the family reunion yet with credentials.

The shoulders of both men relaxed, walls tumbled, fences broken, and ghosts of past expectations, now only comrades—sharers of the grail of grief and life.

"I had to dig for him. It's my inheritance."

With an understanding nod and an old man's whisper, "I heard only yesterday. He was a good man. Kind. I think we'll all miss him." He turned the younger hands back down, reverently. Touching his thumb to the left third finger. "You never married." A statement. An observation. He turned with his embarrassment of having intruded. "I'll get that iced tea for you." Walking down the counter, turning over old memories—weighing the timing and the meaning.

"No, I never did." The soldier sighed as he looked about, taking inventory—the artist's ideal of Miss June sitting astride a John Deere tractor. The calendar was four years out-of-date but smiled and waved to the two years out-of-date Santa waving from his red sleigh. Both seem not to mind the heat, nor the yellowing of their pages as they become older and more anachronistic yet comfortable. "I never found the right one." Or could never have the one I wanted.

Returning, Brice set down the tall "iced tea" in a malt glass, laced with Irish whiskey and a "stake" of mint from outback. It was a "special" only a few ever knew about, and fewer experienced.

"Did you get to see your father… before…?"

Sipping gently, savoring old memories. Liberties shared—served by a rebelling daughter—a metaphor of the forbidden.

"No. He passed quickly." Another opportunity missed. "It was for the best. In his sleep was how he had always wished to go." Another sip, "It's nice when we get our wishes."

"Well, yes, yes, it is that. And I got my wish when my Bonnie came back to live last winter." Leaning against the back-wall counter, right hand rubbing his chin stubble. "Now there's another strange duck for ya. My own flesh and blood. I love her to death, but she never settled down and raised me any gran' ones for my knee ta bounce." Shaking his head slowly in wonder, staring at the floor as if he'd never seen it before. The machinery turned over slowly, as the eyes slowly mopped the floor. His right hand rubbed the drip of sweat on his neck. His voice was far away, almost to himself. "You know… I never knew your name."

"Boudreaux." The long door spring moaned out in the afternoon heat. The western sun glowed warm on the back of the Chaplain's shirt. His back had gone both stiff and soft at the sound of the voice. The high heels clicked once to a stop just inside the door, closing apprehensively.

"His name is Boudreaux, Daddy. David Lafayette Boudreaux."

Her soft voice was embracing kindness and nurture. The gardenia, in her hair, filled the café with the best and sweetest smell summer could offer. All the men in the cafe breathed in deeply.

16

ONE LAST THOUGHT—REALLY

As you can tell, this was never a "How To" book. If anything, it might be close to an explanation about how I write the way I do, where I get my characters, how I build them to be real-ish, and the loose hand of the universe guiding what I write about.

A few things are non-negotiable with me.

There will be animals. Maybe not the ones you expect, but the ones I have experienced. I probably won't get around to putting a gorilla in any of my books, though. But animals have been a large space in my life. Mom said there was another dog before Broadway. But for me, Broadway, a black and white cocker, was my first. Then came the turtle Sunny Jim—who turned out to be a Jane. Cats ate birds, which we fed, so they weren't allowed in our house—until they were.

My sister was babysitting and came home with a handful of fur. Dad barked, and Michaele cried how she was never allowed what *she* wanted. The concession was for *her* to feed and clean *her* cat. And she had to keep it in *her* room upstairs. (To those laughing, shhh…)

About two months later, Michaele was looking all around the

living room and dining room. Mom and I were setting type at the dining table.

Mom looked over her glasses at my sister. Always the sign she already knew the answer. "What are you looking for?"

"Mekong. I'm going to bed."

Mom and I both snorted softly. "Oh, honey. He and your father went to bed an hour ago…"

Yup. That cat was her's no more.

Mekong lived well past twenty. When we moved to a new neighborhood, he systematically went around and beat the snot out of all the dogs. Our two dogs were never molested. They were Mekong's. If it sounds like the cat in my Southside Hooker series, you're close. Box is a blend of Mekong and a big orange tabby named Bucket. The contractor across the street had found him in a bucket on a construction site. He was just as casually assertive as Mekong or Box.

An interviewer once asked, off the record, about there being a gay person in my books.

I looked at her and her long black dreadlocks with a mock shocked look. "There are?"

We laughed and talked about my life. There are also blacks, Latinos, Asians, lesbians, transgender, bikers, truck drivers, nurses, gays, did I mention nurses and librarians. But about my books…

It's not that I'm jaded about the people in my life, but I just don't get the part about not wanting certain people around me, except for those people knocking on my door. No, not the Girl Scouts—they bring the Thin Mints. I meant the other people. The roofers who never look at my aluminum roof before they ask me if I know what condition my roof is in.

I know… You thought I meant the religious people. Hell, nobody wants to see them in the neighborhood. Not once have they showed up with a lawnmower or rake in their hand.

The city I live in, as of this writing, is almost twelve percent self-identifying LGBT. The customers through my shop are a higher percent. The neighborhood is so international that I get to practice at least five languages. It has an effect.

When I finish all the rewrites, polishes, rewrites, pitch and rewrite, polish, readthrough, and my edits—I send my manuscript to the butcher. I dump it in a folder in Dropbox and then go to Facebook. There I leave a message with Rogena, my editor.

Usually, she gets back to me in a couple of days to tell me when she will probably look at it. I move on to any of the other Works in Progress.

I had finished *Pirate's Patch* and did the "dump and notify." *Pirate's Patch* is my soft-core science fiction fantasy. It's about a bunch of immortals who are cleaning up the Pacific Garbage Patch. They are also out to kill one of their similar immortals.

The main character is named for and after a close friend, Blake Stone. Both, like Blake Lively, are female. Mine is Blake Esperanza. She's six-foot-tall. Taller in her knee-high blood-red boots. She has long chestnut hair and loves all kinds of combat—hand-to-hand and up to anything in warfare—it's just a kick-ass romp for fun.

Two weeks went by. No word back.

At the end of the third week, I phoned.

She has caller ID and a special sarcastic hello that oozes out like Mae West. "Heellllooo?"

"What the hell? Did you see the new book?"

"Which one?" Fair game. I'm always working on a few books and an article or six.

I choked. "Pirate's Patch?"

"Oh yeah. Karen (her wife) has it. I'm going to start working on it as soon as she's finished."

"What the fuck is she doing with it? She doesn't read…"

The growl was real. "She read your Stoneheart."

I was caught. "Yeah… Well… But what is she doing with Pirate's?"

She loves it when I'm stuck on the ropes and can't unwind. "Reading it."

"Yeah. I get that. But *why*?" A few years before, Rogena had told me Karen never reads anything for pleasure because she has a massive read load for her work.

She cleared her throat. (It was tough for her to admit.) "Because it's the best lesbian romance I've ever read."

The statement lay in the air for almost a full minute. It wasn't connecting with me.

"Pirate's Patch?"

"Yes, Baer. Your Pirate's Patch."

It still wasn't connecting. "No. It's about immortals. And kicking ass. Tall kick-ass boots. And causing a war. And killing one of their own… and… and…"

I stopped. My voice got ridiculously small. "Oh. Oh yeah… Blake and Christine…"

She laughed. "Really? Your life and friends are so… whatever… You didn't even think about what kind of relationship it was? Maybe we need to move to Portland."

Yeah. My life. My reality.

Don't forget to leave a review. I'm serious. And desperate. Thanks.

ALSO BY BAER CHARLTON

NOVELS

The Very Littlest Dragon: NEW 2019 Editions
(Newly edited editions available: an all-new full-color ebook, a paperback with coloring pages, and a full-color Collector's Edition hardback)

Stoneheart
Pulitzer Nominee 2015

Angel Flights
What About Marsha?
Pirate's Patch
Dry Bridge of Vengeance

SOUTHSIDE HOOKER SERIES
Death on a Dime – Book One
Night Vision – Book Two
Unbidden Garden – Book Three
Boomtown – Book Four
One Day Under the Grass – Book Five

Southside Hooker Series: Books 1–5 Box Set
(Collector's Edition hardback & ebook available)

THORNY WALLACE SERIES
Death in the Valley – Book One
Light to Light – Book Two

—

I Drink Coffee and Make Shit Up

BAER CHARLTON

ABOUT THE AUTHOR

Bestselling author Baer Charlton graduated from UC Irvine with a degree in Social Anthropology, monkeyed around for a while, and then proceeded onward with a life of global travel, multi-disciplinary adventure, and meeting the memorable array of characters he would come to describe in his writing. He has ridden things with gears, engines, and sails, and made things with wood, leather, and metal. He has been stitched back together more times than the average hockey team; his long-suffering wife and an assortment of cats and dogs have nursed him back to health after each surgery.

Baer knows a lot about many things in this world. History flows through his veins and pours out of him at the slightest provocation. Do not ask him what you may think is a simple question unless you have the time to hear a fascinating story.

You can find more at
www.mordantmedia.com

www.ingramcontent.com/pod-product-compliance
Lightning Source LLC
Chambersburg PA
CBHW030323100526
44592CB00010B/548